"Cliff Oberlin and Jill Powers have hit a home run with this **HIGHLY ENGAGING AND VALUABLE BOOK.** Their combination of personal experience and empirical data will help many advisors transform their practice to attract high-end clients. Buy it, read it, and do it. **IT WILL BE ONE OF YOUR BEST INVESTMENTS EVER.**"

STEVE MOELLER
President, American Business Visions, LLC
Author of *Effort-Less Marketing for Financial Advisors*

"Cliff Oberlin and Jill Powers have written a book that should not be on every advisor's shelf. It should be by every advisor's favorite reading chair, on a desk in a quiet room or even at bedside. It should be worn, filled with notes, and perhaps with a coffee stain or two. *Building a High-End Financial Services Practice* is a book to help the advisor think about where and how to direct their business in an increasingly competitive, contentious marketplace. On the fabled shelf, it's worthless. **READ AND TAKEN TO HEART, ITS ADVICE AND INSIGHT COULD SAVE OR MAKE A BUSINESS.**"

BILL GOOD
Chairman, Bill Good Marketing, Inc.

Building a
High-End
Financial Services
Practice

Building a
High-End
Financial Services
Practice

———•••———

**PROVEN TECHNIQUES FOR
PLANNERS, WEALTH MANAGERS,
AND OTHER ADVISERS**

CLIFF OBERLIN and JILL POWERS

WITH A FOREWORD BY JOHN BOWEN

Bloomberg PRESS

PRINCETON

This publication contains the authors' opinions and is designed to provide accurate and authoritative information. It is sold with the understanding that the authors, publisher, and Bloomberg L.P. are not engaged in rendering legal, accounting, investment-planning, or other professional advice. The reader should seek the services of a qualified professional for such advice; the authors, publisher, and Bloomberg L.P. cannot be held responsible for any loss incurred as a result of specific investments or planning decisions made by the reader.

First edition published 2004
1 3 5 7 9 10 8 6 4 2

Library of Congress Cataloging-in-Publication Data

Oberlin, Cliff
  Building a high-end financial services practice : proven techniques
for planners, wealth managers, and other advisers / by Cliff Oberlin and
Jill Powers.
  p. cm.
Includes bibliographical references and index.
  ISBN 1-57660-158-7 (alk. paper)
  1. Financial planners. 2. Financial services industry. I. Powers, Jill   II. Title

HG179.5.O24 2004
332.024'0068–dc22   2003025544

Acquired by JARED KIELING. Edited by CHRISTINE MILES
Book design by BARBARA DIEZ GOLDENBERG

To my parents and my grandmother,
for founding my family's firm
and putting this business in my blood

CLIFF OBERLIN

To my husband and my parents,
for their confidence, patience, and support
of all projects great and small

JILL POWERS

To our partners and the team at Oberlin Financial—
a great group of talented people dedicated
to revolutionizing the financial services world

CONTENTS

Acknowledgments   ix

Foreword   xi

Introduction   1

PART 1 It's Still the Only Constant: An Industry in Change

1   Five Trends, Endless Opportunities   11

PART 2 Your Essential Toolbox: Six Strategies for Success

2   Fewer Arrows, Bigger Targets: 45
     Focus on Affluent Clients

3   Graduating from the Yellow Pad: 61
     Apply the Advanced Consulting Process

4   Build High-Impact Client Relationships: 81
     A Crash Course

5 Take the Wheel: 95
   Don't Let Your Business Drive You

6 E = MC^2, or Education = More Compensation^2:   117
   Commit to Ongoing Learning

7 Building a Deeper Bench: 135
   Forge Strategic Alliances

PART 3 **Mission Possible: Maximizing
Your Broker-Dealer Relationship**

8 The Search for Greener Pastures: 155
   Your Independent Broker-Dealer Choices

9 A View from the Inside: 169
   Evaluating Potential Broker-Dealers

10 Making the Change: 185
    Transitioning to a New Broker-Dealer

11 | Look Before You Leave: 197
Going Independent

12 | A Win-Win Situation: Building a 207
Great Relationship with Your Broker-Dealer

PART 4 **The Future Awaits:
Transform Your Practice**

13 | Pulling It All Together: 215
Design for Success

Resources 223
Index 232

ACKNOWLEDGMENTS

THIS BOOK CAME ABOUT as the result of the encouragement and effort of many people over the years.

First of all, our thanks go to Cliff's father, mother, and grandmother. Earl and Polly Oberlin and Thelma Oberlin-Ford established the core of our client base back in the 1950s and provided inspiration and tutoring for a financial services practice that has thrived ever since.

We are grateful to the late Hy Dolber, who was instrumental in teaching us how to sell investment products, and to Bill Good for teaching us how to build a business, not just create a job. Dan Sullivan showed us how to work on our business, not just in our business. Rick Youssef is a master of life insurance selling who guided us into the world of life insurance.

Without the help of our true friends and founding partners, Tom Hofbauer and Steve Hess, Oberlin Financial would never have become a reality. Ed Reiter, Dave Francisco, Doug Shierson, and Bob Veres have all provided valuable advice and leadership. George Isaac and Pat Hylant are class acts who have long been invaluable advisers to us. Jay Buckingham, one of our board members, really pushed us to go ahead with this book, and for that we thank him. Cathy Eldridge and Dawn Bond have given us top-notch consulting assistance as well as overall sanity retention.

Our thanks go to the broker-dealer and practitioner divisions of the Financial Planning Association (FPA), whose dedication to providing first-class educational and networking opportunities to the financial services industry has been invaluable in introducing us to many wonderful people within FPA and the industry at large.

Cliff is indebted to his sisters, Sue, Salley, and Cyndi, for their steady and ongoing support. He thanks Luke Thaman and Bob Johnson, who taught him how to sell virtually anything so long ago in Junior Achievement, as well as his fellow members of his YPO Challenge Forum, who have been a constant source of valuable guidance and support. His thanks go also to Alexandra Armstrong, one of the founders of the International Association for Financial Planning (IAFP) broker-dealer division, who showed him the ropes in the broker-dealer field, and to Nelson Fleishman, who taught him how Wall Street works. He is also grateful to the Million Dollar Round Table, Top of the Table, and the American Institute of Certified Public Accountants (AICPA) for taking his skill set to the next level through their numerous conferences that allowed him to network with the giants in the industry who are truly the best of class.

Alan Cranfield, Stephen Wolff, Jon Powell, Bill Bachrach, Steve Moeller, and Dennis Clark were all instrumental in getting this book off the ground. Special thanks to John Bowen, who originated the concept for the book, and to Katie Soden, whose writing skills brought it to life.

Our heartfelt thanks go to the entire team at Oberlin Financial, with special thanks to those who have been with us since the beginning, including Denny Harman, Tom Smith, Cheryl Hann, Craig Bavin, Mari Ivan, Jayne Attenweiler, Kylie Rademacher, Bonnie Meyer, Cathy Marchal, Chris Bok, Angie Keller, and Steve Baehren. And last, we thank the network of independent financial advisers who have chosen to work with us.

FOREWORD

THE IDEA FOR THIS BOOK was born on the ski slopes of Utah in the winter of 2001. A group of us, including Bill Bachrach, Steve Moeller, Dennis Clark, and Cliff Oberlin—all self-appointed industry leaders—were spending a week together skiing and hashing out the issues confronting the financial services industry.

We all agreed that we're in the midst of a highly challenging time for financial advisers. Between unprecedented market volatility, new technology hurdles, more (and more complex) financial products, and competition that seems to be coming out of the woodwork, advisers have their work cut out for them.

But at the same time, all of us had seen over and over again in our work with advisers that the ones who are truly succeeding are finding ways to turn all these challenges into opportunities. They know the right strategies for attracting, serving, and keeping the best clients while running their practices profitably and leveraging their strategic partnerships to the fullest. These advisers make it look easy.

For all of us on the slopes that week, a book that set down these strategies in detail seemed like a perfect way to help bridge that gap between what the very successful advisers already know, and what those who aspire to reach huge success need to know. I'm delighted that Cliff Oberlin, along with his colleague Jill Powers, seized the idea and brought that vision to life.

Having built a hugely successful financial advisory practice as well as a thriving broker-dealer, both Cliff and Jill are uniquely positioned to share this message. They know first hand what works today and have a tremendous perspective on what will work moving forward. Most important of all, they both bring a passion to their work of helping advisers create excellence in their businesses as they serve their clients well.

I wish you the best of success.

JOHN J. BOWEN JR.
Founder and CEO, CEG Worldwide, LLC

INTRODUCTION

WITH THE ONSET OF a new millennium and the emergence of a once-every-500-years technological revolution, financial services professionals find themselves poised on a precipice of both immeasurable opportunity and unmistakable uncertainty.

The opportunities today are so great—and the challenges so substantial—that two distinctly different outcomes are emerging for financial advisers.

In the first outcome, the promises of this golden age of the entrepreneur are coming to fruition. These advisers delight in the amazing new products and valuable services they can now provide to their grateful clients. They watch over profitable, highly enjoyable business enterprises. They dream not of retiring, but of pursuing their rewarding vocations for as long as they can.

The second outcome is much different. It revolves around a desperate struggle to manage a mountain of data, a feeling of being chained to an organization, and always floundering one step behind clients who seem to grow increasingly demanding each day.

Which outcome will be yours? Our job with this book is to give you the perspectives and tools you need to make it the first. In some businesses, what you don't know can hurt you. But in our business, it can kill you. This book will help you with exactly what you need to know.

The financial services business has been very good to

both of us, and this book has grown out of our wish to help others realize this same kind of success. We spent many years as advisers (Cliff more than twenty-five, and Jill more than ten) and had the opportunity to build profitable practices working with tremendous clients. We founded and own, in partnership with our network of advisers, a growing broker-dealer that serves top advisers from all over the country.

Although we work now primarily on the broker-dealer side, we've kept our local practice to serve as our "lab"— our proving ground for new strategies to help advisers operate more profitably and better serve their clients. To avoid any possibility of finding ourselves in an ivory tower and disconnected from daily business, our business is built on a horizontal, open-architecture model with few layers of bureaucracy. With this structure, even the people at the top can keep their ears to the ground to know what's happening in the trenches.

All these experiences have given us a tremendous vantage point to see what is working and what is not working for advisers today. We deeply believe that our business holds remarkable opportunities, and our sincere hope is that this book will enable you to fully leverage these opportunities in order to build the business you've always dreamed about.

We've designed this book for three different groups. If you are already enjoying success as an independent adviser, this book can help you move to a higher level of success. If you are just starting out as a financial adviser, this book will serve as a road map to get you on track to building a highly profitable business. Finally, if you are an employee, such as a broker with a wire house, bank, or insurance company, and are considering leaving your firm to pursue a career as an independent, this book will smooth your transition.

We see plenty of good news for independent advisers. With an entrepreneurial character unrestrained by large corporate culture, the independent model is ideally positioned to thrive in our swiftly changing environment. Because they are flexible and able to respond rapidly, independent advisers can leverage shifting conditions well in advance of the large wire houses.

In an industry where the importance of knowing your customers has never been greater, independent advisers are perfectly situated to build strong, profitable client relationships. Free to match their skills and interests to appropriate niche markets, these advisers can become experts in the deep and narrow issues that affect their clientele.

Most important of all, independent advisers have considerable resources available through strategic partners to help them compete successfully and meet ever-growing client demands. Effectively outsourcing a range of tasks and services is becoming pivotal to advisers' success, enabling them to provide clients with sophisticated financial solutions while allowing them the freedom to serve their clients in the best ways possible.

Mixed in with these opportunities are important challenges, however. Once the sole repository of timely financial news and information, advisers are now competing with financial media that seem bent on portraying investing as a mad sprint to the finish. In the atmosphere of urgency created by headlines designed to sell, the solid tenets of long-term financial planning are all but forgotten.

In the midst of what some in the industry call "financial pornography," many investors overlook and even disparage that key quality of so many successful investors in the past: patience. In pursuit of rapid profits, they make near-constant changes in their portfolios to catch the day's hot rising stock or ditch the latest loser. When the market turns down, many show little staying power and exit equities completely, leaving them with poor prospects for ever achieving their long-term financial goals.

As advisers confront this, they also face significant new challenges in running their businesses. Asset management fees for many have dropped to a razor-thin 1 percent or even less. Competition is emerging from unexpected places. Clients are demanding access to increasingly sophisticated—and expensive—technology.

To lead you through all these changes and the best ways to respond, we refer often to industry studies conducted by consulting and research firm CEG Worldwide and its director of research, Russ Alan Prince. We've found this kind of objective, methodical examination of our business to be extremely helpful in identifying trends and successful strategies.

But research will only tell a part of the story. Nothing can replace years of experience or the many lessons we've learned in working with highly successful advisers. For this reason, you'll find stories of what we have seen work in the real world sprinkled throughout the book. We believe this mix of research and experience is a powerful combination for advisers who are serious about excelling.

To guide you through this landscape, *Building a High-End Financial Services Practice* is organized into several parts. In the first, "It's Still the Only Constant: An Industry in Change," we set the stage by describing the most important changes in our industry in recent years, how these changes have an impact on the way advisers do business today, and what the future may bring. Each of these trends holds significant challenges, but also offers substantial opportunities—provided you leverage it well.

In the second part, we show you how to do exactly that. In "Your Essential Toolbox: Six Strategies for Success," we describe the specific strategies you should incorporate into your business in order to capture today's opportunities. We show you how to effectively target affluent investors, implement an advanced consulting process, build client relationships that are profitable in both up and down markets, manage your business for maximum efficiency, undertake lifelong learning that will ensure your success down the road and, finally, build lucrative alliances with other professionals.

In the third part, "Mission Possible: Maximizing Your Broker-Dealer Relationship," we delve into what we consider one of the most critical factors in determining your success or failure: how you choose and work with your independent broker-dealer. We believe the right broker-dealer partner can make all the difference, so in this section we look at your primary broker-dealer choices, how to evaluate a broker-dealer, how to smoothly transition to a new broker-dealer (whether you're an employee about to go independent or are already an independent adviser), and how to obtain the greatest benefits possible from your broker-dealer over time.

The fourth part, "The Future Awaits: Transform Your Practice," will help set you on a course of action for building an elite financial services practice. In it we discuss the importance of creating a plan for change, as well as the steps for successfully implementing that change.

Finally, at the end of the book you'll find a list of resources that we believe will be of great help to you as you move forward in building your business. Whenever we refer to specific programs or people throughout the book, we include complete contact information for them in this section. We've chosen each resource very carefully. We have worked directly with every person we recommend, and over the years working together many have become close friends as well as respected colleagues. We hope they will be as helpful and inspiring to you as they have been to us.

PART 1

It's Still the
Only Constant

An Industry
in Change

There's little doubt that we're in the midst of a revolution in the financial services business. We see five major trends under way that are rapidly redefining how you serve your clients, with whom you compete, the tools you use, and what you have to do to succeed. These trends will continue to shape our industry for many years to come.

These changes are converging to create a defining moment—a watershed—for our industry. They could well mark the beginning of the end for those advisers who do not adapt in response. We believe that those advisers who cling to older business models and technology will likely survive only through sheer will power and daily grind.

Conversely, the advisers who adapt to these changing

conditions by taking full advantage of the new tools and opportunities they offer will not merely survive; we expect them to thrive and enjoy a level of success most advisers in the past could only dream about.

To avoid being overwhelmed by events, it's important to understand why these trends are happening, where they'll take us, and how you can capitalize on them, both for your own profit and to better serve your clients. In this first section, we look at the trends we see as having the greatest impact on our industry today and point out the incredible opportunities they hold for advisers.

CHAPTER 1 # Five Trends, Endless Opportunities

TREND 1
The Rise of the Rich:
The Growth of Affluent Client Markets

As YOU'LL SEE throughout this book, to reach a high level of success as an adviser you must work, at least to some degree, with affluent clients. Fortunately, this market is large and getting larger, and the affluent both need and want to work with financial advisers.

Worldwide Expansion of the Affluent Market

According to the *World Wealth Report 2002,* published by Cap Gemini Ernst & Young and Merrill Lynch, there are more than 2.2 million people in North America with financial assets of at least $1 million, not including real estate. Their asset wealth totals some $7.8 trillion, a number estimated to grow by more than 43 percent to $11.2 trillion by 2006.

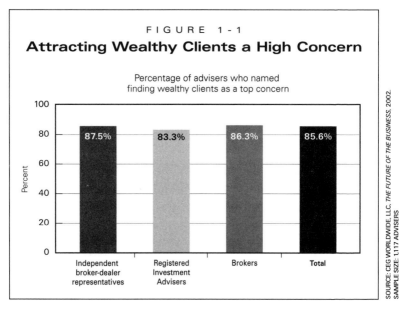

FIGURE 1-1

Attracting Wealthy Clients a High Concern

Percentage of advisers who named
finding wealthy clients as a top concern

SOURCE: CEG WORLDWIDE, LLC, *THE FUTURE OF THE BUSINESS,* 2002.
SAMPLE SIZE: 1,117 ADVISERS

The trend is similar worldwide. There are currently 7.1 million individuals around the globe with assets in excess of $1 million, with total assets of $26.2 trillion. It is expected that the assets of these high-net-worth individuals will grow by 8 percent annually to reach $38.5 trillion by the end of 2006.

This growth in the affluent market is matched by a desire on the part of these investors to work with financial advisers. The large majority of affluent investors at all levels are either completely or partly dependent on financial advisers to manage their assets, and as their net worth increases, they become even more inclined to seek such help.

As the opportunities to work with the affluent market are growing, so too is the competition among advisers for these investors. A study from research and consulting firm CEG Worldwide tells us that large numbers of advisers of every kind make finding wealthy clients a business priority.

As **FIGURE 1-1** shows, 85.6 percent of all surveyed advisers cited attracting affluent clients as a top concern in their businesses.

This concern is shared by all major advisory channels, with overwhelming majorities of independent broker-dealer representatives, Registered Investment Advisers, and stockbrokers all focused on finding wealthy clients. Among independent broker-dealer representatives, attracting the affluent is the single highest concern, outranking even apprehensions about the market going down or concerns about generating asset growth.

The Accessible Affluent
Too often advisers think that the affluent market is out of their reach. To help dispel this myth, let's set out some definitions of the different levels of affluence, in terms of investable assets:

- **Mass affluent:** $100,000–$999,999
- **Significantly affluent:** $1 million–$4,999,999
- **Super affluent:** $5 million–$24,999,999
- **Ultra affluent:** More than $25 million

The mass affluent are actually a huge market, consisting of millions of "ordinary" people. This market is probably richer than you may have thought, as well as much more accessible.

We believe that the significantly affluent market—investors with between $1 million and $5 million to invest—is a very sweet spot for many advisers. For the elite advisers, it's their bread and butter. The super affluent and ultra affluent groups obviously offer even greater opportunities for the top advisers wishing to expand yet further up market. With complex tax issues and a multitude of solutions to choose from, these investors are increasingly dependent on financial advisers to guide them.

Unfortunately, it's nearly impossible to just start with the significantly affluent, super affluent, or ultra affluent. You *must* start with at least the mass affluent, however. If you're working with clients on a long-term, in-depth, consultative basis, you simply can't keep the promises you make to them regarding quality service if these investors have less than $100,000. Reporting requirements alone are now so extensive that it is becoming very costly to carry small customers.

(If you were determined to work with clients with less than $100,000, you would have to use a model that is much different from what we describe in this book in order to be successful. You could not hope to offer any level of customized, personalized service; would have to be extraordinarily technologically efficient; and have legions of clients. Although this may be a viable business model for some advisers, it's clearly outside the scope of this book.)

Of course, it can make sense to occasionally make exceptions to this rule when doing so promises to pay off in the future. For example, when we consider prospects for our local practice, we look not only at how much an investor has right now, but also where that person will be down the road. A promising young entrepreneur, for instance, may not have significant investable assets, but has a lucrative career ahead. Likewise, someone working in his family business may only be earning $50,000 a year right now, but eventually stands to inherit a profitable venture. We believe it can be smart to go ahead and work with these kinds of investors, knowing that they are very likely to become one of our affluent clients in the future.

Complex Needs Require Sophisticated Services

When it comes to working with financial advisers, affluent investors are squarely in the driver's seat. They have many different financial professionals competing for their business and have their pick of advisers. With so many advisers focused on the affluent market, it's obvious that not all will succeed. The race is going to be won by the advisers who have a deep understanding of these investors: who they are, the products and services they need, and how they want those products and services delivered.

Affluent clients are quite willing to pay for financial services when they perceive that they're receiving value. The greater these clients' assets, the more opportunities advisers have to truly demonstrate their ability to add significant value. But you can't expect to offer garden-variety, mass-market solutions to these clients and still expect to succeed. What works for the mass market simply won't deliver the kind of value the affluent are looking for.

The affluent have complex and interrelated needs, including wealth enhancement, asset preservation, wealth transfer, and charitable gifting. Each of these involves, to varying degrees, expertise in the investing, tax, legal, and regulatory arenas. To work successfully with the affluent, you need to have sharp interpersonal skills and a stable of reliable resources—either among in-house staff or other financial professionals—that you can tap when needed.

One affluent family that our local firm works with is typical in its range of needs. We began by providing the family business with a profit-sharing plan, but expanded over the years to include money management, life insurance, financial planning, estate planning, a range of trusts, and a family foundation. This family has many different highly specialized needs and absolutely requires a firm that can provide or access expertise in all of them.

Along with these kinds of intricate needs have come higher expectations for quality service. Over the last decade, we've seen affluent investors grow much more knowledgeable about their financial options, putting greater demands on advisers to constantly remain on the cutting edge.

We've also seen the affluent become much less inclined to automatically take everything advisers say at face value. They're looking for more options and expect detailed explanations for the reasons behind them. You need to be prepared, starting with your initial presentation, to justify your recommendations and explain their ramifications. With many affluent clients, you'd better be prepared to do this in a specific, technical manner.

Think about it: Doctors, lawyers, engineers, and successful business owners didn't just stumble into their professional positions. They're all used to reading the fine print (like legal contracts, business plans, and prospectuses), making client presentations, and being held accountable for delivering the results they promise. You won't be able to sing and dance your way into the trusted-adviser circles of these investors simply by showing a flashy PowerPoint presentation. These investors are sophisticated businesspeople in their own right and generally won't stand for working with anyone they perceive as less than an expert. You need to know your products, know your costs, and know every detail, inside and out.

Besides questioning the specifics, we've also seen affluent investors grow more particular about the overall approach of entire firms. They're not willing to use a firm simply because their parents did (in fact, we've seen many cite this as enough reason to *not* use a firm). Instead, they want to see new strategies that are adapted specifically to their own needs.

This means you will have to perform a bit of a balancing act. You must distance yourself from the "old school" approaches of years gone by and position yourself on the leading edge of technical expertise and capabilities. At the same time, you have to be seen as well established, thoroughly knowledgeable, and absolutely trustworthy.

Between providing the sophisticated services the affluent need, positioning your firm to attract the affluent, and offering the world-class client service the affluent demand, you're faced with a huge challenge. But in our experience, the advisers who can surmount this challenge have a much greater upside potential than all other advisers.

When you work with the affluent, you can have fewer clients, yet earn more. It gives you the opportunity to solve complex financial challenges, which helps you build a reputation as an expert. You gain insights from working with astute clients who demand innovative approaches, keeping you always on top of your game, and you avoid the burnout faced by so many advisers who are strictly product salespeople. For us, all of this adds up to create enjoyable, stimulating careers and great personal satisfaction.

We strongly believe, however, that the demands of the affluent are simply too great to be addressed by any single adviser. To be successful at attracting and keeping wealthy clients, you must outsource the activities that are beyond your core competencies, either to other advisers within your firm or to experts outside of your firm. As we discuss later in this chapter, outsourcing can give your affluent clients both the top-shelf service and financial expertise they need.

TREND 2
The Geek Wars:
The Revolution in Technology

THERE IS NO LONGER a single facet of our business that is untouched by technology. It has penetrated every function at every level of every firm and is used to some degree by every person in every office.

Like it or not, how well you are able to leverage the benefits of technology while minimizing its pitfalls has a great deal to do with how successful you will be as an adviser. To do this, you must have a clear understanding of where technology is today and where it's likely to go.

Promises and Challenges

At its best, technology can enable you to focus on what you do best—your core competencies—rather than on administrative or operations tasks. It can be of incredible assistance in delivering high-quality client service, and doing so very cost-effectively. It can reduce staff costs by increasing productivity and work pace. By providing sophisticated portfolio research, management, and reporting tools, it can elevate the quality of recommendations that your clients receive.

Of particular interest to independent advisers, technology holds the potential to level the competitive playing field, providing you with efficiencies and information that will allow you to more easily compete with the wire houses.

These advantages and opportunities, however, come with substantial challenges. As you move ahead in implementing technology, these are the basic problems that you'll need to find ways to overcome.

Lack of compatibility. A huge technological barrier is the inability of many different programs to communicate with one another. This requires tedious and time-wasting duplication of client data entry into various applications. For example, many contact management systems are terrific tools for keeping in touch with your clients, but few of them allow you to pull account data from multiple sources (although this problem is being remedied by some vendors). This means you need to enter the data manually and then update them manually every time there's a trade in the client's account. Thus, getting your contact management data to interface with your portfolio management system just adds one more layer of complexity to the task.

Lack of development. We have found that many products simply do not live up to the claims made for them. Although they will do particular tasks perfectly in a vendor demonstration, their performance in real-world application is often less rosy. Many advisers are eager to implement additional technology but are hamstrung by this lack of development.

Lack of breadth. Some products are touted by their vendors to be all things to all advisers, but experience has taught us that few, if any, actually are. They may perform one or several tasks very well, but fail to be the one-stop solution that most advisers really need.

Expense. The high cost of some programs is an outright barrier for some advisers. For others, it's difficult to accurately evaluate in advance if a program's contribution will justify its cost. Until a program is installed and running, it's impossible to know with certainty that it will perform as advertised or that it will integrate smoothly with other systems in the office.

Constant need to upgrade. Besides being a significant expense, upgrades can cause compatibility problems when a newer program will not work in conjunction with another, older program.

Inadequate support. The level and cost of initial training and ongoing support vary from product to product. Although support is excellent in some cases, it often is not. As a result, we find that with some programs, advisers end up not using the entire menu of features that is offered—and that they paid for. CEG Worldwide's research echoes this, reporting that fully one-third (33.7 percent) of all advisers identified a lack of training in technology as a significant obstacle to their success.

Technology's Future

Technology today is much like a teenager: a bit clumsy, subject to mood swings, making mistakes that can be very expensive, and full of bright potential. From technology's adolescent haze, however, we see several important things clearly emerging about its future that will have a big impact on your business.

Investment in technology will not be a frill. An adviser's failure to invest in technology may lead directly to a loss of market share. At the very least, it will lead to a loss of productivity and new opportunities.

No solutions are perfect, nor will they be anytime in the near future. Despite this, advisers cannot afford to wait for perfection. They must begin to incorporate technology as much as possible in order to be poised to move ahead.

The gap between needs and tools will remain. The expectations of both clients and advisers of what technology ought to be able to do will always be several steps in front of what it is actually able to do. Technology developers and industry regulators will always be scrambling to keep up.

Although some standardized products used throughout the industry are bound to emerge, advisers will always be faced with weighing their best options from a selection of less-than-optimal products.

The technology divide will widen. There is an ever-growing gap between the advisers who have gone to great lengths to integrate technology into their businesses and the advisers who adopt new technology only reluctantly or not at all. As technology continues to expand in importance, those who are committed to leveraging new tools will move forward, whereas those who are slipping behind will fall behind even further.

Because deploying technology wisely is so critical to your success, we talk much more about how to do it in Chapter 5, "Take the Wheel: Don't Let Your Business Drive You."

TREND 3
The Enemy Within, Without, and Wherever: The Rise of Competition

IN TODAY'S hypercompetitive marketplace, just working harder isn't enough. To beat the competition, you must know your opponent. You need to clearly grasp how your competition is evolving and what to expect in coming years so that you can structure your business to respond effectively.

The (Not So) Good Old Days

For some perspective, let's glance back a few years to see how much competition has changed. Independent advisers have always had tough competition for their clients, but just ten years ago the landscape they faced was drastically different from today's.

Back then, the big wire houses did a great deal of cold calling, pitching their "Stock of the Day" or "Fund of the Week." They succeeded with this approach because the public at the time seemed much more inclined to regularly do business with cold callers.

We're reminded of a very good client of ours who had an appointment scheduled with us to invest some additional money that he had accumulated in savings. He had a fairly conservative portfolio, with several municipal UITs and bond funds and a small portion in growth and income funds. When he called to cancel his appointment, we were puzzled and asked him if there were any problems. "No," he calmly informed us, "a nice young man from New York called me on the phone the other night at home, and he has offered to let me buy a very good stock that he knows about." We were floored! We were lifelong friends with this gentleman, but he was willing to give his money to a stranger who phoned him from New York. With the increase in telemarketing fraud over the last decade, we're fortunately now seeing substantially less inclination on the part of investors to do business with a cold caller.

We also saw a good deal of competition from career life insurance agents who sold investment products, as well. The big insurance companies had huge sales forces in the field devoted to soliciting our clients. In addition, they had enormous advertising budgets that allowed them to create high levels of brand loyalty. This marketing did much to increase the perception of value and legitimacy by consumers, and these companies thrived because of their name recognition. Individual advisers simply had nowhere near that kind of brand identity.

As a result of all this different competition, many clients had incredibly piecemeal portfolios, put together with no real thought to asset allocation or overall strategy, and often held in a number of different accounts spread among their advisers, wire houses, and insurance companies. For some investors, this was their idea of "diversification."

So although competition ten years ago was intense, it gave us an advantage we no longer have: It was easy to know who our competition was, what they were selling, and how they were selling it. Now, all that has changed.

Competition on Many Fronts

For an idea of the many facets of competition today, let's look at a survey done by CEG Worldwide in May 2001. This study asked 716 advisers—most of them independent representatives affiliated with broker-dealers, but also including some Registered Investment Advisers

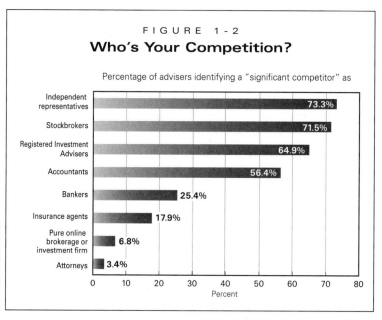

FIGURE 1-2

Who's Your Competition?

Percentage of advisers identifying a "significant competitor" as

Independent representatives	73.3%
Stockbrokers	71.5%
Registered Investment Advisers	64.9%
Accountants	56.4%
Bankers	25.4%
Insurance agents	17.9%
Pure online brokerage or investment firm	6.8%
Attorneys	3.4%

Percent

SOURCE: CEG WORLDWIDE, LLC, *MAXIMIZE THE BOTTOM LINE*, 2001.
SAMPLE SIZE: 716 ADVISERS

(RIAs) not affiliated with broker-dealers—to name their most significant competitors. As FIGURE 1-2 shows, nearly three-quarters (73.3 percent) of these advisers saw their primary competition as themselves—other independent representatives.

Stockbrokers from the wire houses ranked second, at 71.5 percent, followed by RIAs, who were named by 64.9 percent of those surveyed as significant competitors. These responses are much as we would expect, and confirm that our traditional competitors are still very much a factor. However, you would be making a costly mistake if you assumed that the competition stops there.

The Invisible Competition

In recent years, we've started to see advisers losing business to firms that they previously didn't even consider their competitors. This competition is nearly invisible—until it takes your clients away.

A prime illustration of this is the new competition we're seeing from some banks. Not so long ago, banks were just places where our clients kept their checking accounts. Beyond monthly account statements, banks didn't actively communicate with their customers, so we never gave them a thought in terms of competition. Now, however, banks are starting to offer a myriad of investment services, and often in ways that are difficult to anticipate.

For instance, we work with an adviser who recently lost a pension account to a bank headquartered in a distant city, one that doesn't even have a branch in his area. He had no way of knowing that this bank had begun soliciting his clients and was doing business in his area. By the time he realized with what he was competing, it was too late.

The Explosion of Investing Noise

An even more difficult kind of competition to fight is the onslaught of investment coverage by the media. Between hundreds of Internet sites, a range of cable television channels devoted exclusively to investing, and magazines screaming urgent headlines ("Five Mutual Funds You Must Buy Now"), advisers are competing with a deluge of data and opinions.

We believe that investors' decisions can only be as good as the information on which they base those decisions. Although certainly some of the information investors can access these days is quite good, much of what we see and read is simply hype—noise, not useful information. The various media outlets are in fierce competition themselves, and the headlines that sell the most are those that are most sensational, sometimes even outrageous. The most eccentric commentators—those forecasting the Dow at 500 (or 40,000)—are the ones who get the airtime. For the most part, investors still see the press as generally unbiased.

The real danger for investors is that this level of investing noise just feeds the inclination of so many to move quickly and not fully consider the consequences. Attention spans are short and the media have infused the investing atmosphere with urgency, making clients crave almost constant change in their portfolios. In up markets they fear missing out on the hottest new investment, whereas in down markets they fear staying too long with that same investment. So when a media pundit suggests something that looks reasonable to them, they'll go after it immediately.

The sheer amount of information available has also blurred the distinction between bad and good advisers and made inexperienced investors feel like market experts. Knowledge has been confused with wisdom.

Years ago, financial advisers had access to most of the information and doled it out to their customers as they saw appropriate. These days, the customers can sit at home (or work) for hours on end transfixed by the investing websites or cable news networks, being spoon-fed the latest fast-breaking gossip, rumor, guess, or outlandish comment that the reporters gathered that day.

Having access to this information and quoting it ad nauseam will make you *appear* smarter than before you had access to the information at all. But using all that information to make truly profitable decisions has proven to be much more elusive, both for clients and financial advisers.

We've seen clients move to advisers who clearly over-promise results and, even worse, who cloud the real issues with bad data. Ultimately, they do their investors a major disservice. Meanwhile, the good advisers must fight through the haze of bad ideas and advice just to be able to present their own recommendations.

We're also seeing a strong push toward action—any action. We hear clients saying, "Do something, do *anything.*" The buy-and-hold strategies of the past are losing their appeal in our society of instant gratification. Increasingly, investors believe that investing is like driving—if they are not actively managing their portfolios, they are asleep at the wheel, bound to crash. To many, the idea of sitting, waiting, and hoping that things will get better is like a lamb being led to slaughter. To them, taking control of their finances means getting in and getting out, changing and exchanging.

The Me E-Generation

Finally, we've observed a significant shift in clients' attitudes toward their abilities to direct their investments them-selves. We call this the "me e-generation"—all the people who say, "I can do it myself, and I can do it online."

Make no mistake; we applaud investor education and empowerment. Online tools are an incredible resource for those relatively rare investors who set sensible, long-term courses and then manage their investments wisely through changing market conditions.

More often than not, however, we've seen the Internet only exacerbate the tendencies of investors to move too quickly, trade too often, and operate without a long-term investment strategy. It seriously oversimplifies the complexity of financial services and seriously underestimates the role psychology plays in investor decision making.

A case in point: We know one investor who made his living as a personal fitness trainer. He spent his days in the gym with his well-to-do fitness clients who would often offer him investment tips. While his clients were working out on the treadmill, he watched television, tuned into CNBC or CNNfn. Armed with this information, he started actively trading online. As could be expected, his portfolio was devastated in very short order, and a significant portion of his hard-earned wealth was lost.

Let's face it, the fundamentals of solid, long-term investing are boring. To win against the competitors who flourish on a short-term, transactional approach, you have to convince clients of the value of committing to a long-term investment program. We describe exactly how to do that in Chapter 3, "Graduating from the Yellow Pad: Apply the Advanced Consulting Process." You also have to educate clients so that they can set realistic expectations for their investments, which we talk about in Chapter 6, "$E = MC^2$, or Education = More Compensation^2: Commit to Ongoing Learning."

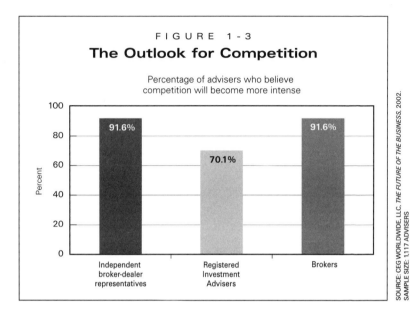

FIGURE 1-3

The Outlook for Competition

Percentage of advisers who believe
competition will become more intense

SOURCE: CEG WORLDWIDE, LLC, *THE FUTURE OF THE BUSINESS*, 2002.
SAMPLE SIZE: 1,117 ADVISERS

The Competition Ahead

What competition does the future hold? Looking across
the different adviser segments, the study represented in
the figure above finds that by far the majority of all advisers
believe that competition will grow stronger. Independent
broker-dealer representatives and stockbrokers overwhelm-
ingly hold this view, with more than 90 percent of both
groups seeing competition increasing in the future. (See
FIGURE 1-3.)

In our experience working with a range of advisers, we've
found that those at all levels, including highly successful
advisers at the top of our industry, take their competition
extremely seriously and look for ways to provide a higher
perceived value to clients and prospects moving forward.

In looking at how the competition will play out in terms
of how many advisers will survive, research finds that a solid
majority (72.0 percent) of surveyed independent broker-

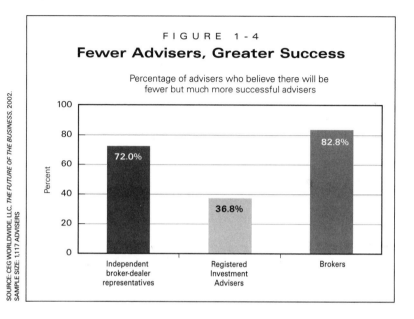

FIGURE 1-4

Fewer Advisers, Greater Success

Percentage of advisers who believe there will be
fewer but much more successful advisers

SOURCE: CEG WORLDWIDE, LLC. *THE FUTURE OF THE BUSINESS*, 2002.
SAMPLE SIZE: 1,117 ADVISERS

dealer representatives believe there will be fewer advisers in the future, but that those remaining will enjoy greater success. (See **FIGURE 1-4**.)

From all of this, we can pull threads of hope. As we've already seen, serious investors, particularly the affluent, are extremely interested in working with competent advisers. We go into detail on how to attract wealthy investors to your practice in Chapter 2, "Fewer Arrows, Bigger Targets: Focus on Affluent Clients."

Even more important, there are advisers who are finding ways to buck the competition and succeed despite it. These advisers understand what they need to do to not just survive in this environment, but to thrive and build highly profitable businesses. We point out what makes these advisers tick, and how to incorporate their best practices into your own firm.

TREND 4
What I Can Do, You Can Do Better:
The Ascent of Outsourcing

ADVISERS OPERATING out of a one-person shop can no longer expect to meet a broad range of client needs entirely on their own. Instead, the most successful advisers rely on networks of other professionals to provide the services they need that are outside their own area of expertise. To understand how to best leverage this trend, we look at why outsourcing has become so important and how highly successful advisers are using it.

Outsourcing's Evolution

Just ten years ago, outsourcing was in its infancy. Financial products were much simpler, clients' needs were generally more straightforward, and most advisers operated on a clear-cut product sales basis. We were trained to sell a single product to handle all needs, so we had few reasons to outsource additional products. We did relatively little comprehensive planning—clients would come to us with a portion of their money, and we would put it to work within our product-based format.

No longer. The needs of clients, the products that have been developed, and the regulations governing these products have all grown in complexity by leaps in the past decade. Savvy advisers have realized that this complicated environment requires them to be more diligent in their recommendations and to seek out the best possible advice. When advisers sense that a particular product increases their liability exposure, they're much more inclined—as they should be—to bring an expert into the process. They understand that without this level of diligence, it would be far too easy to sell a product assuming that it does one thing, when in fact it could end up doing something else entirely.

We're seeing this particularly with some of the products that are geared for the affluent market. Smart advisers understand that simply jumping into selling a hedge fund, for example, without being an expert on the complexity of that product or consulting with someone who is, would leave them wide open for trouble. They would run the risk not just of unhappy clients, but also of legal action that could threaten their ability to stay in business.

In addition, the intense market volatility of this turn-of-the-century period has convinced more and more advisers that they need a broad stable of products to draw upon to meet different needs during different markets. A particular product may not work in today's market, but might be extremely useful tomorrow. They understand that a great deal of the value they can add for clients comes from choosing and blending a number of very different products. To provide this wide range of products—and the accompanying expertise—they are turning to outsourcing partners.

Finally, the investing public itself has grown to understand that no single person can know everything about every product and service. Every investor wants to work with an expert. In many ways, this has raised the bar for all advisers, requiring them to have specialists to whom they can turn for this expertise.

From our perspective, the most successful advisers already fully appreciate the necessity for outsourcing and are quickly making it a part of their businesses. They understand that to compete well and stay happily in business over the long term, they have to make the best possible use of their time and skills. They've asked themselves, "What is the best and most cost-effective way to provide this product or service?" Very often, their answer is to outsource it.

By focusing on their core competencies, they create a true win-win situation for themselves and their clients— they are able to spend their time on the activities they most enjoy and where they best excel, while their clients receive high-quality service and the advice of experts in their specialties.

Conversely, we see many other advisers who have yet to learn the importance of outsourcing. There are still large numbers trying valiantly to provide for all client needs by themselves. These advisers like to retain control over every aspect of every process, mainly because they believe that no one else can do the work better. They do not want to acknowledge—either to themselves or their clients—that they lack expertise in any area. Rather than being an expert in even one area, however, these advisers achieve just mediocre knowledge in many areas.

Although this structure is what these advisers want, it's extremely hard to grow this kind of practice. They end up plateauing in their growth and then burning out. Ultimately, it's extremely difficult for them to sell their practices because the values of their firms are wrapped up entirely in them. These advisers have jobs, not businesses.

Looking forward, this trend toward ever more outsourcing shows no sign of slowing. Products will only grow in their complexity, alternative investments and strategies will continue to evolve, and the needs and expectations of clients will keep expanding. As outsourcing becomes even more important, we believe that the divide between advisers who understand the need to outsource and those who do not will grow even wider.

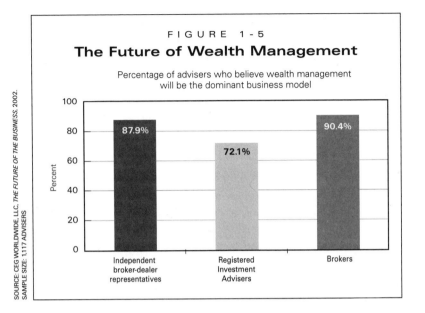

SOURCE: CEG WORLDWIDE, LLC, *THE FUTURE OF THE BUSINESS*, 2002.
SAMPLE SIZE: 1,117 ADVISERS

FIGURE 1-5

The Future of Wealth Management

Percentage of advisers who believe wealth management
will be the dominant business model

Chart values:
- Independent broker-dealer representatives: 87.9%
- Registered Investment Advisers: 72.1%
- Brokers: 90.4%

Wave of the Future: Wealth Management

The growing importance of wealth management—
the integrated process for helping clients manage wealth
on a consultative basis—provides a prime example of the
need to outsource. CEG Worldwide's research gives us a
clear indication of how important wealth management will
be to advisers and their clients in the future. As **FIGURE 1-5**
shows, large numbers of every type of financial adviser see
a bright future for wealth management.

With its diverse set of complex services, including
everything from investment consulting and alternative
investments to insurance, estate planning, charitable giving, and trust and mortgage services, wealth management
demands that advisers outsource. Affluent investors looking
for wealth management services are not interested in being
sold a proprietary product formula. What they do want is
to work with advisers who deeply understand their needs

and can work with a range of specialists to find and tailor
the best-of-class products to meet their highly specific situations. These investors know full well that a single adviser
(or even a single firm) cannot provide the expertise in all
the areas they require.

To provide this level of service and range of products,
you need to work in ways that allow you to focus on your
core skills and then leverage the talents of others by outsourcing everything else. These outsourcing partners may
be entirely outside of your firm (if you're a sole practitioner) or, if you work in a multiple-practitioner firm, they
may be both within and outside of your firm. What matters
more is that these experts are the best that you can find,
able to offer better, more creative, and more competitive
products than anyone else.

The Outsourcing Model

To understand how successful advisers are making outsourcing work, think of a continuum with pure asset management at one end and pure relationship management at
the other. Every adviser and specialist has a place on this
continuum according to his skills, expertise, and interests.

The pure asset manager typically works within a specialty,
such as money management, retirement planning, financial planning, or life insurance. These advisers do no selling
and may not even work directly with clients, but instead rely
on others to bring them assets. To these advisers, *what* they
know is most important.

At the other end of the scale is the relationship manager, who never directly manages assets, but instead selects
the specialists who will. These advisers are like gatekeepers
standing in the middle of a large room with many doors:
They choose which doors to open when, bringing in the

resources that will give them the best possible solutions. To these advisers, *who* they know is most important.

Relationship managers may also work closely with other professional advisers, such as accountants or attorneys, who in turn work with their own teams of specialists. These advisers consult with one another on overlapping issues and often frame strategies to work in concert with one another.

The client is at the center of this web of relationships. As the focal point, the client enjoys long-term, consultative relationships with his or her advisers, as well as the best-of-breed products and services that those advisers bring to the table from their experts.

Obviously, neither asset managers nor relationship managers can succeed without the other. Asset managers can be excellent technicians, but without relationship managers to bring them work, they have to divert at least part of their efforts away from their core expertise and onto sales. Likewise, relationship managers can have superb people and management skills, but without a solid network of competent asset managers to whom they can outsource, they can't focus on what they do best.

Because sales always tend to earn more than service, the relationship managers are at the more profitable end of the continuum. These advisers are the ones meeting with clients, and ultimately that is what shows up most on the bottom line.

But there is still plenty of room for success at the other end of the continuum, provided asset managers have the links with relationship managers that they need. We see asset managers succeeding either within multiple-practitioner firms such as ours that have in-house relationship managers, or within single-function firms that have established solid contacts with other firms that send them business. Either way, the asset managers are fully dependent on relationship managers to drive their sales.

Depending on the size and structure of your firm, you can even fit somewhere in the middle on the continuum, working to some degree as both asset manager and relationship manager. (This is what stockbrokers in the old days used to call a "customer's man.") To achieve a high level of success in this position, however, you still must rely on others at either end of the continuum.

Outsourcing as a Single or Multiple Practitioner

Is it better to implement this model as a sole practitioner or as a multiple practitioner? It depends entirely on your circumstances, talents, likes, and dislikes. Some people prefer the independence of a sole proprietorship, without the obligations that come with having partners or the responsibilities that come with having employees. Others enjoy managing employees and are able to juggle those duties in addition to their primary work. Still others are happy to trade the uncertainty of owning their own business for the security of being an employee.

What is more important than how you structure your firm is your ability to attract work from relationship managers (if you're an asset manager) or to locate top-notch asset managers (if you're a relationship manager). It matters relatively little whether your sources are under the same roof or scattered around the country, as long as you have them.

One adviser who is a member of our broker-dealer is a great example of how a single practitioner can leverage the outsourcing model. With a passion for meeting people and forging meaningful connections with clients, she is a pure relationship manager. She has a cadre of experts to whom she outsources all needed financial services, including specialists in financial planning, money management, and insurance.

She operates in an office-sharing environment with relatively little overhead, has very good revenues, and realizes a healthy profit every year. Best of all, she's doing exactly what she enjoys most and is best at doing: building relationships and gathering assets. Because she outsources everything outside of this single core competency, she has a high quality of life and extremely satisfied clients.

In our local practice, it made the most sense for us to use a multiple-practitioner structure. Because of our location in northwest Ohio, it's much easier and less expensive to recruit and train an employee here than it would be in, say, New York or San Francisco. If our business were in either of those cities, we would outsource specialized tasks much more often.

Your Outsourcing Partners

Pure relationship managers working as sole practitioners will, of course, need to outsource all of their asset management work. But even relationship managers working within multiple practitioners will need at times to look beyond members of their own firms to find precisely the expertise they require. There are two major kinds of outsourcing partners to whom you can turn.

Strategic partners. Your strategic partnerships can range from informal referral sources to deeply entwined and formalized alliances. These kinds of partnerships are extremely important to some of our industry's most successful advisers and, we believe, will grow more important in the future. We will look in depth at how to identify potential strategic partners and build successful alliances in Chapter 7, "Building a Deeper Bench: Forge Strategic Alliances."

Institutional partners. You can outsource some tasks to your product sponsors, such as your mutual fund and insurance companies. An asset management company can also be an important outsourcing partner, as can your clearing firm. Because it also allows you to outsource key functions and offers you a number of support services, your choice of broker-dealer is perhaps the most important thing that determines whether you achieve serious success. We look at each aspect of the broker-dealer relationship and how to make the most of it throughout Part 3, "Mission Possible: Maximizing Your Broker-Dealer Relationship."

TREND 5
All Together Now:
The Increase of Consolidation

THE FINAL TREND influencing the way advisers must do business today to succeed is the acceleration of consolidation throughout our industry. For many advisers, this may seem like a trend that is usually far-removed from their own day-to-day practices, yet it actually affects many aspects of their businesses, and provides significant opportunities.

Fewer, Bigger
The financial services industry over the last decade has experienced significant consolidation, as organizations like large, often multinational, banks and insurance companies have acquired independent broker-dealers. To a lesser degree, there have been notable mergers of broker-dealers, creating even larger broker-dealers that in turn have been acquired by banks or insurance companies.

In any case, the parent company is generally not a broker-dealer, so creating profitable partnerships with financial advisers is not its core business. For advisers, this means that the decision makers that ultimately affect their businesses—the parent companies of their broker-dealers—may know very little about what they do, who they serve, or what they need to be successful.

The Ups and Downs of Consolidation

For independent advisers, this trend is a double-edged sword, offering both drawbacks and advantages. On the downside, advisers may find that their broker-dealer has become a cog in the wheel of a larger business plan. It is operated with an eye not toward what is best for the broker-dealer (and in turn, the advisers that it works with), but toward what is best for the parent company.

It can also have a substantial effect on advisers' marketing efforts, coloring their clients' perception of objectivity or service. Where clients once saw an independent business designed for taking care of their specific needs, with a large merger or acquisition they can begin to see a large, faceless, uncaring organization.

We experienced this ourselves shortly after our previous broker-dealer merged with a large bank holding company. When one old friend sold his business and invested the proceeds with another adviser, he told us, "I would have given you the money to manage if you still had your business, but now that you're with the bank, you're not unique anymore." This person assumed that, being part of a larger organization, we would no longer be able to give him the personalized, customized service he desired.

We can also pull some threads of good news for advisers from the increase in consolidation, however. For instance, there are now more opportunities for advisers who are just beginning their careers and want the security of being an employee within a large company. It's not at all unusual for advisers to start out as representatives at banks or insurance companies in order to learn the trade. Although they won't have all of the freedom of an independent adviser, they will get all the resources and training that large companies can provide. They'll get a row to hoe, and they'll learn a lot. It can be an excellent training ground for those advisers who eventually want to go independent and start their own businesses.

Consolidation has also resulted in some important economies of scale that can be advantageous to independent advisers. This is true particularly in the area of technology, where development is extremely expensive but deployment to large numbers of users is relatively cheap.

Finally, we believe this trend has encouraged the growth of small, niche broker-dealers. (We founded our own broker-dealer, for example, in response to consolidation.) These small broker-dealers can carefully target a select group of advisers to serve, very often, the highly successful, elite advisers. For these advisers, this means the potential for high-quality, profitable partnerships with broker-dealers that understand their unique needs and design their firms to serve them well. This match of top advisers with niche broker-dealers is highly advantageous for both partners.

PART 2

Your Essential Toolbox

Six Strategies for Success

Years and years of hard work can build your business, but pure hard work alone won't take you to the elite level. You need tools, partners, and efficient ways of working, otherwise there will simply never be enough hours in the day to make your business a success. Eventually, rather than owning your business, it will own you.

Because just working harder won't get you there, you have to work smarter. To help you do this, we've identified six primary strategies, each one designed to help you grow your business by capitalizing on the trends we discuss in Chapter 1.

We've developed these strategies by combining our experience building a successful retail practice with our experience working with other top advisers through our broker-dealer. Over the years, we've had many opportunities to fine-tune each strategy, making it as effective as it can possibly be in creating positive change in your business.

In this section, we'll take an in-depth look at each strategy, showing you why they all can help you grow your sales and enhance your service, and describing exactly how to successfully implement them in your practice.

CHAPTER 2 # Fewer Arrows, Bigger Targets: Focus on Affluent Clients

W E OFTEN SEE ADVISERS putting huge efforts into getting new clients—any new clients—with the mistaken belief that additional clients will automatically translate into a higher income. In contrast, we believe that to build a healthy, more successful practice, you're likely to need *fewer* clients than you have today, not more.

To make it with fewer clients, however, you must have the right kind of clients—the affluent. (In Chapter 1, we define the affluent as those clients with at least $100,000 in investable assets.) By shifting your emphasis from getting *more* clients to getting *more profitable* clients, you'll have the time you need to build strong relationships and provide high-quality service. This in turn will lead to higher client retention, more referrals, and a healthier bottom line.

Certainly it is possible to succeed with a large number of clients. We know several advisers with thousands of clients

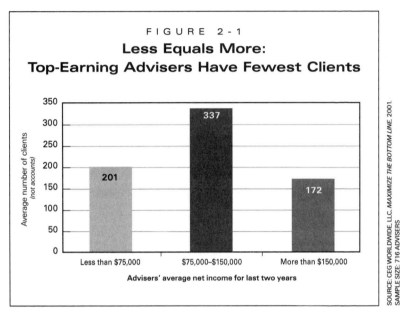

FIGURE 2-1

**Less Equals More:
Top-Earning Advisers Have Fewest Clients**

SOURCE: CEG WORLDWIDE, LLC, *MAXIMIZE THE BOTTOM LINE*, 2001.
SAMPLE SIZE: 716 ADVISERS

and huge staffs who have figured out how to run their operations efficiently enough to be successful. But increasing their scale often has not increased their income. With their very high overhead, they are earning no more than other advisers working as sole proprietors or in small firms with far fewer clients.

This corresponds with research from CEG Worldwide, which finds that advisers earning the highest incomes actually have the fewest number of clients. As you'll see in **FIGURE 2-1**, the surveyed advisers with at least $150,000 in annual income had an average of 172 clients. Advisers earning between $75,000 and $150,000 had 337 clients, or nearly twice as many. Even advisers in the lowest income group had more clients—201.

We understand that working with the affluent isn't for everyone. Some advisers are more comfortable working with moderate-income clients and have built rewarding careers helping these investors. Everyone has a different personal definition of success—and for these advisers, it may not include making a lot of money.

But if your idea of success includes building a highly profitable business, and you are comfortable working and socializing with the affluent, then you absolutely must work with wealthy clients. The general affluent market is probably much more accessible than you may assume, and includes investors with as little as $100,000 in investable assets.

We look at two key things in this chapter that will help you capture a slice of the affluent market:
- what the affluent want from their advisers
- how to turn wealthy prospects into clients

What Do the Affluent Want?

IN OUR WORK with wealthy clients, we hear one thing from them more than any other: "We want to make sure we're doing the smartest possible thing with our money that we can do."

This simple statement gives us a glimpse of the essentials the affluent are looking for in an adviser. Let's look at each one:

They want an adviser they can trust. Confidentiality ranks very, very high for the affluent. They need to know that the information they share with you will be guarded and used only in appropriate ways. With many clients, you'll need to earn this trust every step of the way.

We are always taken aback when we hear "trusted advisers" talking about their clients or dropping names of prospects at social gatherings. When Cliff was attending a breakfast meeting one morning with a number of business owners, he heard another adviser talking about a client's affairs.

The person seated next to Cliff turned to him and said, "I certainly hope he's not going to talk about me next."

The affluent do not want their business discussed publicly. We can guarantee that no matter how large the community is in which you operate, this type of indiscretion will come back to haunt you. Respect their need for privacy and do not violate their trust. Your outsourcing resources must, of course, do the same.

They want an adviser who truly knows them. The affluent understand that you will not be able to help solve their challenges unless you have a fundamental knowledge of who they are.

To work with truly elite clients, you will need to understand their values and goals, empathize with their problems, and excel at providing timely advice—and not just financial advice.

Remember, the affluent can go to anyone for financial advice and solutions. One of the best ways you have to really stand out from other advisers is through the relationships you establish with these clients. As we've heard over and over, these clients are saying, "I want you to know who I am."

Our own success with many of our affluent clients is largely founded on our close relationships with them, which go much deeper than simply that of financial advisers. Our role includes equal parts of peer, mentor, neighbor, and sounding board. They are often looking for advice on more than just their investment portfolios, so we make it a high priority to continually get to know them and their needs even better.

We've also seen affluent clients who want their adviser to essentially be on their own personal board of directors, ready to offer advice on a range of issues. For instance, they might want guidance on how to raise capital for a business,

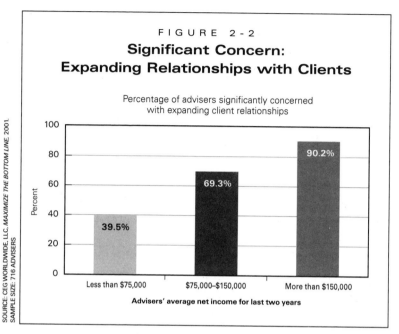

FIGURE 2-2

Significant Concern:
Expanding Relationships with Clients

Percentage of advisers significantly concerned
with expanding client relationships

39.5%

69.3%

90.2%

Less than $75,000 $75,000–$150,000   More than $150,000

Advisers' average net income for last two years

SOURCE: CEG WORLDWIDE, LLC. *MAXIMIZE THE BOTTOM LINE.* 2001. SAMPLE SIZE: 716 ADVISERS

strategies for buying out a business partner, advice on setting up a trust for their children, or direction on starting a personal or family foundation. These are all personal issues, and affluent investors need a trusted adviser with whom they can discuss them.

CEG Worldwide's research clearly shows that most successful advisers understand the importance of building client relationships. When asked about significant concerns in their businesses, the overwhelming majority (90.2 percent) of top advisers named expanding relationships with their clients. This compares to just 39.5 percent of lower-income advisers. (See **FIGURE 2-2**.)

They want expertise. The affluent rightly see their financial needs as complex, requiring sophisticated solutions. Accordingly, they want deep expertise in every area of investing and planning that affects their situations.

Fortunately, they don't expect you to provide all of that expertise. They understand that no single adviser can be an expert in every area of financial services (and would be skeptical if you said you were), but they do expect you to be able to refer them to professionals in areas outside of your specialty who can provide the additional expertise they need. They also want you to be able to work effectively with these professionals in order to provide comprehensive solutions.

They want you to believe in what you sell. You must authentically believe in the investment or strategy yourself or you won't be able to sell it successfully. When you really don't know all that you should know about a concept, or don't quite believe in it yourself, you can sing and dance all you want, but your message won't ring true, and the client will know it. If you're a younger adviser, anything you recommend should pass the "parent test." Ask yourself: "Is this an investment that I would put my parents in?" If the answer isn't "yes," you won't sell it successfully—nor should you try. (Likewise, if you're an older adviser, put everything to the "kids test.")

They want custom-built solutions. The affluent want the choices and services you offer to be fresh, elite, and custom-designed for their specific situations. They want to know that financial solutions are built just for them, not for the mass market.

A perfect example of this desire for customization can be found in a large private company that is a client with our local firm. The owners of the business approached us to make a proposal to them for a pension and profit-sharing plan. They had been through a number of different providers in the previous several years and clearly were quite knowledgeable on the subject. After we made our presentation, they called and essentially said, "We've had that kind of plan before. You're going to have to do better." So we went back to the drawing board and worked with outsourcing partners to design an entirely new, customized profit-sharing model from the ground up. The business owners decided to use the plan, and it has since become one of our most successful and exciting offerings, and one we're quite proud of.

They want value. The affluent are quite willing to pay for your service, but only when they perceive that their money is well spent. They want advisers who will use their resources wisely, and love to hear about how you cut corners to save them money (without cutting service, of course).

Don't assume that simply because clients are wealthy they don't love a discount. Without fail, on ski trips with some of our biggest clients and prospects, a major topic of discussion is who uncovered the best airfare and who scored the best rental car deal. Each of these people has a net worth in excess of $50 million, and yet is still determined to save a few dollars on vacations.

Trying to surpass the lifestyle of your affluent clients is a mistake. Not only can it lead to personal financial problems, it can be a real turn-off to these clients, who are not interested in seeing you live well on their money. A professional appearance is important here, but live within your means.

They want an adviser with passion. Finally, the affluent want you to share their own drive and determination for achieving their financial goals. Let your dedication, enthusiasm, and love for your work show through in everything you do.

Cliff once made a presentation to a client who immediately followed his recommendations. One week later, the client came back, bringing his college-age grandson.

He asked Cliff to make his presentation again because, as he said, "I wanted my grandson to hear your presentation because you deliver it with such passion. I wanted him to see that he needs to have that kind of passion in any career he enters."

Reaching the Affluent

HAVING THE RIGHT expertise, products, approach, and attitude are all essential for working successfully with affluent clients; however, they are not enough to send wealthy prospects your way. You need to find effective ways to reach out to these investors, using methods that are aligned with how they prefer to be contacted.

The advisers we know who are successfully marketing to the affluent have done one or both of the following:

They have established relationships with affluent prospects—in nonprospecting circumstances. These advisers have created opportunities to build quality relationships with well-to-do investors. For example, they may serve on the board of directors of a nonprofit organization together, participate in the same community service organization, or simply have been introduced by a mutual friend for a round of golf. The actual situation matters little; what does matter is the chance to spend one-on-one time so that adviser and prospect can get to know one another in a friendly, nonsales atmosphere.

In no case are these advisers using these circumstances to deliberately attempt to sell their services. Instead, they are building a network of relationships with a community of wealthy investors. Invariably, these relationships will result first in one referral, and then, as the adviser proves his or her worth, a steady stream of them.

They have established relationships with professionals who work with the affluent. In the same way that they build relationships with affluent prospects, these advisers cultivate contacts with professional advisers who work with these prospects, most often accountants and attorneys. In time, these relationships lead to valuable referrals.

We see these types of professionals as extremely important to adviser success. Unlike individual clients who, at best, might provide a handful of referrals, professionals provide a valuable entrée into extensive networks of people all working with the affluent. These partnerships are so important, both for driving new sales and for outsourcing services, that we go into much greater depth about building them in Chapter 7, "Building a Deeper Bench: Forge Strategic Alliances."

CEG Worldwide's research echoes our own experience in this area. One study that shows the extent to which different prospecting strategies are used by more and less successful advisers is quite revealing. As you can see in **FIGURE 2-3**, the

SOURCE: CEG WORLDWIDE, LLC. *MAXIMIZE THE BOTTOM LINE.* 2001.
SAMPLE SIZE: 716 ADVISERS

FIGURE 2-3
Prospecting Strategies

STRATEGY	ADVISERS' AVERAGE INCOME FOR LAST TWO YEARS		
	Less than $75,000	$75,000–$150,000	More than $150,000
Cold calling/direct mail/observation	39.9%	21.3%	5.2%
Word of mouth and client referrals	46.2%	57.2%	79.5%
Referrals from other advisers	0.9%	16.0%	43.8%
Seminars	31.8%	42.8%	32.1%

top-earning advisers relied primarily on referrals, both from clients and other advisers. The lower-income advisers, conversely, had much less success getting referrals, particularly from other advisers.

Put yourself in the shoes of a wealthy investor: How would you find a financial adviser? Would you respond to a cold call or direct mail piece? Of course not. Would you attend a seminar? Possibly, but only if it were targeted to your specific needs and circumstances, and not simply open to the public.

More likely, you would reach out to your network, asking for referrals from your friends and colleagues. You would talk to your attorney and accountant in order to tap into their networks of professionals. Because you would seek referrals from people like you and from professionals who know you well, you would be highly likely to locate an adviser who is well suited to assist with your particular financial needs.

The advisers who are a part of these broad networks of the affluent are in an optimal position. Through their relationships they can derive a flow of referrals for clients who, by virtue of their membership in the network, are already prequalified. Because of their own contacts within the network, these clients in turn become a valued referral source, assisting friends and clients in locating professional advisers in other areas.

These relationships don't happen by accident. You need to build them, systematically and deliberately. In our own work, we have found that there are three key tactics for building these kinds of relationships.

1. Be Intentional About Working with an Affluent Community

Before anything else, you need to be clear about your intentions to work with affluent clients. To reach the affluent, your challenge is to be deliberate, narrow your focus, and consciously choose to specialize in a niche market dominated by wealthy investors.

We see advisers make two fundamental mistakes in their marketing efforts. First, some advisers jump around, targeting many different markets but never fully committing to any one. When they stumble on one marketing strategy that does work, they tend to change it, and it no longer works. They operate tactically, trying many different marketing approaches in the hope that they'll work. They never give enough thought to which market would be most profitable or how the people in that market would actually like to be reached. As a result, they never become well known to a single community of prospects.

Second, other advisers carefully target a particular market, building their expertise and cultivating relationships within that market, but still fail to make a good living. The reason is that they go after the wrong markets—those without a lot of money. We've found time and again that advisers tend to earn about what their clients earn. If you don't target wealthy prospects, you yourself will probably not become wealthy.

In contrast, when you establish yourself within a niche community of wealthy investors, you realize important benefits:

- You are able to focus on activities that have the highest payoff.
- You become an expert in that group's particular set of financial challenges.

- Your name becomes recognized as the adviser of record for that community.
- As a recognized expert within the community, you receive more referrals from both clients and other professional advisers.

2. Identify Your Ideal Niche

The next step is to choose your best-suited niche, or narrow target market. Niche opportunities are everywhere, but you have to do some research to uncover the ones that may be right for you. This is a profile of the ideal niche:

- The niche is aligned with your skills, talents, and interests.
- The niche has a high concentration of qualified prospects with significant investable assets who are able and willing to pay for your help.
- The individuals in the niche share a similar set of values, challenges, and goals.
- You would enjoy working and socializing with the people in the niche.

Examples of potentially profitable niches abound: top-level people in a particular industry (for example, pharmaceutical company executives), professionals from one field (for example, dentists or radiologists), or even people devoted to a particular sport or hobby (for example, skiers or sailors). Regardless of your choice, you must be passionate about what you do and be able to explain it quickly and clearly.

Our own market niche consists of successful, wealthy entrepreneurs. We have extensive backgrounds in business with large and small companies, both public and private, and so we have a great deal in common with this group. In addition, we attend seminars frequently, so we are bombarded with lots of new ideas that we are able to pass on to clients. Cliff has his own foundation, so he understands very well how private foundations work. He also has a great deal of coaching experience, which is useful in working with the affluent. Most important, we work with this group successfully because *we are part of the group*—we understand its challenges intimately and are able to provide solutions that work.

In identifying niche opportunities, don't be afraid to follow your passions. Do you love golf? Skiing? Then find ways to combine these activities with your work. You'll have that best of all worlds: doing what you love to do, working with people who share your interests, and being paid well to do it.

When starting to build key relationships, don't overlook your existing client base. Who are your favorite clients? Are they part of a wider group that offers opportunities? If so, ask them to introduce you to others in the group. Identify individual prospects. Talk to centers of influence that work within the group, such as community and business leaders. Set the foundation for strategic alliances by contacting attorneys and CPAs who work in the niche.

In short, you'll need to do a lot of good, old-fashioned networking, and in an extremely focused and targeted manner.

3. Establish Your Place Within the Niche

Get involved. Draw yourself into the niche community, truly becoming a part of it. Build a rapport with people and be 100 percent sincere about it. Attend social functions and cultivate friendships. The more involved you become with the community, the more people you will meet to work with, which will give you even more reason to become even more deeply involved.

Become an expert at solving the financial challenges of your niche community. By understanding the challenges and opportunities of the niche group, you will be able to provide unique or compelling benefits that provide substantial value to the group. Gather the specialized knowledge you need to work effectively in those areas. Remember that many affluent people view financial specialists merely as product pushers. You do not want to be perceived by the niche as someone simply selling products, but as the person with the expertise to meet their distinctive challenges. This is your ideal position, and it is a very powerful one.

Cultivate referral networks. Whenever you are already known by a prospect through a third party within the niche, whether that is a client or another professional adviser, you have a huge head start in building that relationship. Your credibility will be assumed without you having to demonstrate it. Referral sources put their own reputations on the line when they refer you, so be the reliable, trusted adviser they assume you will be. In turn, you should constantly look for opportunities to give back to your referral sources by way of your own referrals.

Build your credibility. Highly educated professionals are always looking for timely information that will increase their wealth of knowledge. Fill this need and increase your credibility by writing articles for trade or association publications read by people in your niche. Publish and distribute your own newsletter focused on the financial challenges and solutions of the group. (This newsletter must be entirely your own creation and specific to the needs of your target community, not a boilerplate sent out by dozens of other advisers.) Take advantage of any public speaking opportunities within your niche community.

Whenever you see a newspaper or magazine article that addresses the business or investing concerns of an individual in your target niche, clip it out and mail it with a note that says, "I thought you'd find this to be of interest." Likewise for any investment research you receive that pertains to people in that community.

Brand yourself. It's important for you to have a clear brand identity to help you stand out to affluent prospects from the mass of other advisers. If allowed, build your own business name, rather than using that of your broker-dealer. This has become particularly important in this era of consolidation.

Be able to tell your story. Affluent prospects will want to know who you are and what you stand for before they consider giving you business. Be able to tell your story, and be known as someone with a story.

Perfect the art of listening. Many people in our business value the art of talking, but careful listening is what is truly powerful. People enjoy talking about themselves and are flattered and impressed when you recall what they've told you about themselves. Listening intently in order to discern real priorities and problems will get you much further in your community than the most polished sales pitch.

Don't push and don't promise more than you can deliver. So many people are after the business of the affluent that these investors are put off by aggressive salespeople. We've seen pushy advisers occasionally make initial sales (more often than not by wearing down the prospect or by promising results that they could not possibly deliver), but we have never seen one establish a productive, long-term client relationship. Do not abuse your place in the community by employing aggressive sales tactics.

Involve them in your success. If someone in your niche community gives you a hand up, acknowledge it, thank her, and remain in close touch. People who help you, like mentors or confidants, will have a stake in your success and will be important backers to you throughout your career.

CHAPTER 3 # Graduating from the Yellow Pad: Apply the Advanced Consulting Process

A S YOU'VE SEEN in Chapter 2, affluent clients are looking for some very specific things from their financial advisers. They want someone they can trust, someone who genuinely knows and understands them, someone who brings a high level of expertise to the table, and someone who can provide them with customized recommendations. And they want all of this to be a good value.

This is a tall order. Fortunately, there is a proven process that meets each of these needs. The advanced consulting process will enable you to earn your clients' confidence; identify their real, long-term goals and values; and design expert, comprehensive solutions. It will also allow you to systematically demonstrate the value you bring to their financial lives.

In this chapter we look at exactly what it means to use this consultative approach, including:

- the benefits it can bring to both you and your clients.
- who among your clients and prospects is right for this process.
- how to implement the advanced consulting process in your practice.
- how to make a smooth transition to consulting.

A Better Way to Do Business

WITH SO MANY people calling themselves consultants these days, it might be easier to define the advanced consulting process by what it is not. It's not "yellow pad planning," where an adviser asks a client a few questions, jots down notes on a yellow pad, and makes an on-the-spot recommendation for certain products. These advisers are reacting, following a road set out for them by what their clients want.

A lot of us were taught to sell something to our prospects first and then make them clients. If you take this traditional approach, you immediately position yourself as a salesperson. There is nothing wrong with being a salesperson, but you won't be seen as that trusted adviser clients are looking for when you position yourself this way.

Instead, when you use the advanced consulting process, the client follows the course that *you* set. You use a defined process that will uncover your client's needs and goals, formulate a comprehensive solution, and then monitor and adjust the solution on an ongoing basis.

There are huge advantages to doing business this way. First, it will help set you apart from all your competitors who are focused on simply making the sale. Your clients won't see you as just another financial services vendor, but as a partner in their financial lives. Because you'll

SOURCE: *MARKETING MUTUAL FUNDS THROUGH INDEPENDENT ADVISERS.* RUSS ALAN PRINCE AND DARLENE DEREMER, 2001. ANALYSIS: CEG WORLDWIDE, LLC. SAMPLE SIZE: 1,419 ADVISERS.

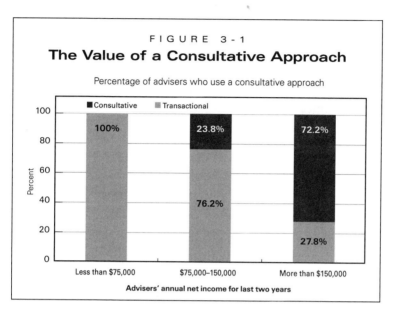

FIGURE 3-1

The Value of a Consultative Approach

Percentage of advisers who use a consultative approach

know much more about clients' overall financial pictures, you'll know where they have additional assets and, as you build the relationships, you'll be in a great position to ask for—and get—those assets. By building strong and on-going relationships with clients and earning this position of trusted adviser, you'll also find it much easier to get referrals.

Obviously, all of this can add up to more income for you and your firm. A study of independent advisers by CEG Worldwide shows what a dramatic difference this approach can make to an adviser's bottom line. As you can see in **FIGURE 3-1**, almost three-quarters (72.2 percent) of the highest-earning advisers in the study used a consultative approach. In pointed contrast, every single one of the 1,419 surveyed advisers making less than $75,000 used a transactional approach.

Finally, the way you approach the advisory process

totally impacts your quality of life. If you're product-driven, you've got to get up every morning and make a sale. But when you use a fee-based consulting process (which we define as receiving more than 50 percent of your compensation in fees) and have money under management, you get to lead a much more planned, relaxed, and balanced life.

Going to a Fee Basis for All the Right Reasons

HAVING SAID ALL THIS, we do want to caution you against moving to fees just for the sake of being fee-based. Being paid through fees can be nice, but don't get so caught up in it that you forget it's just part of delivering the kind of service affluent clients want and expect. If you're motivated to convert to a consulting process solely because you believe you'll end up earning more money, you're missing the point.

Instead, we suggest that you concentrate on deciding the best way to work with each particular client. When working on a fee basis enhances and supports the consultative nature of your relationships with certain clients, and you're convinced that it's the best possible move for helping them achieve their financial goals, go for it.

But if you feel that other clients are better served and more profitable to you by remaining on a commission basis, don't pursue converting to fees just to be paid by fees. How much money you end up making has a lot less to do with how you charge your clients than it does with how well you take care of them.

CEG Worldwide backs us up on this point. Its research into how advisers view transitioning to a fee-based business

SOURCE: CEG WORLDWIDE, LLC. *MAXIMIZE THE BOTTOM LINE*, 2001.
SAMPLE SIZE: 716 ADVISERS

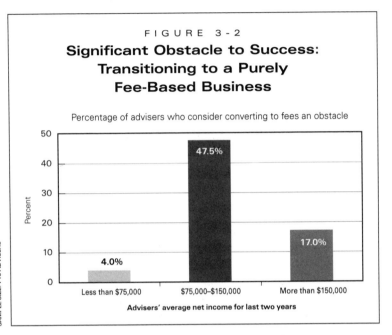

FIGURE 3-2

Significant Obstacle to Success: Transitioning to a Purely Fee-Based Business

Percentage of advisers who consider converting to fees an obstacle

Advisers' average net income for last two years

shows that the most successful advisers—those earning more than $150,000 a year—really don't care much about being fee-based. But among advisers earning between $75,000 and $150,000, almost half (47.5 percent) saw converting to a fee basis as a major obstacle to their success. (See **FIGURE 3-2**.)

In our own local practice, we are paid by both commissions and fees. Although we prefer to work on a fee basis when it makes sense, we know that it's not right for every client. But the mechanics of how we are paid is not really the point. What's more important to us is being fairly compensated and delivering value to our clients. As long as clients understand the value we're bringing, they nearly always see it as equitable, too.

The Right Clients for the Process

WHEN YOU WORK with clients on a consultative basis, you're going to have to do a lot of work for each one before you ever realize any revenue from them. This means you can't work on a fee basis with just any client who walks in the door—you need to make sure it's the right client. To distinguish between the clients who should be on fees and those who should be on commission, do a quick cost-benefit analysis for each one.

The first thing to look at is the amount the client has to invest. To make it worth your while with smaller clients, you really have to work on commission. If the client has such a small amount to invest that you'll end up making no money (or even losing money) by switching to fees, you're not doing anyone any favor. We know some fee-only advisers who hate turning work away so much that they will take on some of these smaller accounts. They consider work with these clients as pro bono and keep them in hopes that they will one day be the source of a big referral. Accordingly, these advisers provide less service and monitoring for these accounts as compared to their more profitable clients.

This makes it challenging for advisers just starting out to work on a fee basis. For these advisers, a better course is often to remain on commission while building their client bases, and then start to convert once they have clients with whom they can profitably work on a fee basis.

So who is the ideal client to work with on a consultative, fee basis? Look for four different things:

They are interested in receiving your advice over the long term. They are sophisticated enough to understand the value of a coherent, long-term approach and don't

treat you as just a commodity or a means to getting trans-
actions executed. Nor are they simply shopping around
for a new adviser.

They have plenty to invest. This means they will be profitable clients you can afford to keep for many years.

They understand the value you deliver. They don't think
that they are doing you a favor by working with you and
won't beat you up every quarter about your fees. They don't
mind paying you an ever-increasing fee because they know
the service they receive is well worth it.

You would enjoy working with them. Since you'll be
spending time with them over the long term, they need to
be clients you like and respect, and who like and respect
you in return.

It's easy to overlook the last point when you're eager
to take on new fee clients. We learned how important it
really is years ago when we got a call from a prospect interested in investing a settlement he'd just received from a
major wire house. It turns out that this person had successfully sued not just one, but two, major brokerage houses
after investments they had recommended dropped in
value. We made the mistake of working with this client, but
it was never much fun. The client recorded every conversation we had, implying that we'd be the subjects of another
lawsuit if we were not extremely careful. Once we realized
our mistake, we suggested that he move on to a new adviser.
We will never work with this kind of client again, no matter
how much we might earn.

The Advanced Consulting Process

THE CONSULTING PROCESS we recommend has six distinct elements:

1. Presentation of Capabilities

You'll first outline exactly what your firm is capable of doing for the prospect (or prospects, if you do the presentation in a group setting). You'll describe what your firm is responsible for and what prospects are responsible for, should they decide to become clients. You'll set expectations, letting the prospects know just what you do and how you work. You'll also explain how you are compensated, describing both fees and commissions.

It's important for you to create a system that makes these presentations flow smoothly. In our firm, we use a binder of material that stresses our capabilities and that lets us customize for a particular presentation or audience. We suggest you create a script that tells your story and rehearse it in advance.

We've seen sales made and lost by a turn of phrase, so spend time to get your presentation right. If you don't yet have much public speaking experience, consider videotaping your presentation and having it critiqued by a public speaking specialist. These experts can help you identify the small (or not so small) hitches in your presentation, like that nervous twitch, the interminable "ahh's," poor pacing, or a monotone delivery. There are also some amazing tricks of the trade for everyone that differ by sex, age, and physical presence that such a specialist can teach you.

It's also very important to get agreements of understanding (called "tie-downs") at every stage of the presentation. Check to make sure that your audience is still with you by asking, "How does it sound so far?" or "Does that make sense?" Address them directly by name whenever possible. We've seen so many advisers just keep talking and talking, oblivious to the glazed eyes of their audience. Not only do they lose their prospects' attention, they lose the opportunity to address concerns or answer questions the audience may have.

As part of your presentation, you should prequalify prospects, determining whether they are candidates for your services. Have some questions ready that will help you drill down to what they really want and the best way to deliver it. You want to find out what truly motivates them, what they value about money, and where they want to go with it. If it helps, you can prepare a script for these questions. Either way, the key is to be a very good listener at this point.

If the prospects seem like a good match, walk them through your entire process, describing what will happen at each step. Explain that the next step will be for you to gather the information from them you'll need to formulate your recommendations for their specific needs. The reason for doing this is you want them to have faith in the integrity of your process. It's much easier for prospects to make a decision and a commitment when they understand that you have a consistent, high-quality system in place.

2. Discovery

During the discovery step, you'll define prospects' financial needs, goals, and current positions, and collect the information you need to make your recommendations. We've found that using a questionnaire is the best way to do this. This approach is easy—it's amazing what people are willing to share when someone across a table asks them questions from a form—and it ensures that we get complete information on every client.

Don't restrict your questions to the usual nuts and bolts about investments they currently own. Ask broad, open-ended questions that will help you uncover as much as possible about their situations and the opportunities they may hold for you. Our own questionnaire, for example, includes these questions:

- What was your best investment ever? What was the worst?
- Are you still working? If so, what's your occupation?
- Do you have children? If so, what are their ages and occupations?
- What are your life goals?
- Why do you invest?
- Who is your CPA? Your attorney?
- Do you have a will or trust? Is the trust funded?
- What are your hobbies?
- What clubs or organizations do you belong to?

Questions like these help us define what's important to the client, let us know about bad financial experiences they might have had that we should avoid, and tell us a lot about other opportunities for working with the client (such as in estate or insurance planning) that we might otherwise not know about.

In particular, work to know about other assets the client has but is not yet ready to let you manage. Explain to the prospects that it's important for you to know about their entire portfolio in order to avoid replication and recommend the proper allocation. Tell them that you'll build a balanced portfolio based on what you know, but if they have assets that you don't know about, they won't get the best possible recommendations. Be sure to mention if it won't cost them anything extra for you to include these as part of your suggestions.

Be aware that many investors, particularly the affluent, believe that no one adviser can provide all the answers. They're going to want to keep those other accounts so that they can continue to receive multiple opinions. Regardless, make it your job to try to know as much as possible about their complete picture.

3. Diagnostic Meeting with Other Advisers (Optional)

This meeting is typically held in conjunction with the prospect's CPA, attorney, and/or insurance agent. This professional is preferably a strategic alliance partner with whom you work, or could also be the prospect's "personal chief financial officer" who manages every aspect of her financial life and who has called you in to provide assistance in a particular area.

At this meeting, you would present your diagnosis of the investor's situation and goals with a summary of your recommendations. You'd gather any additional information that influences the prospect's position so that you could adjust your recommendations as needed. You would establish a general agreement with the other advisers about the direction you are suggesting. Because you'll hash out any disagreements you may have regarding strategies or recommendations, it's preferable for the prospect to not attend this meeting.

Although this step is a tremendous way to solidify the prospect's financial strategies and put all her advisers squarely on the same team, we've found that investors are often reluctant to authorize this kind of quarterbacking. They don't want to pay for the extra time that would be billed by the other advisers, or they may not yet be willing for you to be privy to their entire financial situation. In these cases, you can skip this step.

4. Present Recommendations

At this stage, you'll present your recommendations to the prospect. Depending on what she has told you she needs and wants, this recommendation could be quite broad or very narrow. It might take the form of a financial plan; an investment policy statement; your suggestions for a specific service, such as a 401(k) plan for her company; or something else entirely.

Always use visuals, such as a PowerPoint presentation, to help explain and illustrate your recommendations. Include general educational materials that support your recommendations that the clients can take home. (Let them know in advance that they can take this material home so that they can listen and don't have to spend time taking notes.) Throughout your presentation, be specific about the next steps the client should take to move ahead.

Because you're not working on a product-driven, transactional basis, this is where it becomes so critical to have access to other professionals, either within or outside of your own firm, who can provide you with the capability you need in developing recommendations in areas outside of your core expertise.

5. Secure the Agreement

Now review your recommendations and answer any questions the prospect may have. Address any objections or reservations, and make any adjustments as necessary. Encourage the prospect to act immediately to make his decision.

Ideally, your hard work now pays off when you get a firm commitment and the prospect becomes a client. In anticipation of this, have the paperwork ready that you'll need to open accounts and transfer assets. To expedite this step, we always have the paperwork partially filled out in advance.

At this point, your value is fresh in the client's mind, and he is firmly committed to working with you. Take advantage of this by asking for referrals of other investors who could benefit from your help. Ask the client, "Do you know anyone I should be talking to?"

6. Establish Ongoing Contact

Once your client is on board, set up a schedule for being in touch with him regularly. Ask him how he wants to be contacted and how often. Some clients will want a quarterly meeting as a matter of course, but others will want you to call only if something is wrong or needs to change. Sometimes your largest clients will want the least contact—we have one with a $10 million account, for instance, who wants us to check in just twice a year, and only once in person.

Regardless of how frequently you meet with clients, cover these essentials at every meeting:

Update the clients on their investments. Review their investments' performance, tell them about any changes, and answer any questions. We've found one very effective way to do this is to first ask the clients for their perception of how their investments have been doing, and then review the actual performance in the context of both their perspective and the appropriate benchmarks.

Uncover changes in their financial situation. Ask, "Did anything significant happen in your life since we met last?" This will help you make adjustments as needed, and will pinpoint new opportunities for you. If the client has recently experienced a job change, for example, or the death of a close relative, chances are excellent that she has a new financial need that you can meet.

Ask about any service issues they have. Check your service log on the client before each meeting. If you have your service team built the way you should, you'll never hear about minor service problems. However, if an issue has arisen, the client may well be unhappy, but still reluctant to bring it up to you. By asking every time about service-related problems, you'll ensure ongoing satisfaction.

Educate the clients. Reinforce to them the value of the comprehensive, long-term process that they've engaged in, particularly when the markets are down. Warn them about chasing performance, and talk to them about the underlying costs of trading often. (We look much more closely at the issues you should address with your clients in Chapter 6, "E = MC^2, or Education = More Compensation^2: Commit to Ongoing Learning.")

Continue to ask for referrals. When you meet with your top clients—those you enjoy the most and who are most profitable—ask them if they know anyone who would benefit from your services. If you've built a consulting process that is consistently delivering a great value to these clients, you shouldn't hesitate for a moment to ask them for referrals. More often than not they'll be happy to help.

Ask for additional assets. Because you probably won't know about all of a client's assets, you need to consistently work at uncovering assets you are not yet aware of. (We've found that a client's tax return is the single best way to do this.) If you see a new asset that looks appropriate for you to manage, ask if it can be transferred to you.

When asking for other assets, be sensitive to the fact that clients may have relationships with other professionals that are so important to them they insist on leaving some assets with that adviser. We work with one client, for example, who owns some mutual funds sold to him by one of his golf buddies. We know about these assets, but would never suggest that he move them because we understand that his friendship with his golf partner would prevent him from doing so. We wouldn't want to displace this relationship, so we simply remember to consider these funds when evaluating his portfolio. We figure that whatever we might lose in fees is more than made up by goodwill and referrals. Quite often we eventually end up with all their assets, anyway.

Refining Your Process

ONCE YOU HAVE the framework for your consulting process in place, you should continually fine-tune it to make it as effective as possible. There are four things that have been especially useful to us in making our consulting process run smoothly and profitably.

Adjust the Process to Match Lifestyles and Personalities

Depending on each situation, this process might go very quickly or be spread out over some time. For clients with large, complex accounts who have time to meet with you, you should devote an entire meeting to each element. We've found that for old money in particular, the process itself is very important, and it pays to have it unfold step by step.

More often, however, you'll find you need to accelerate the process to fit people's lifestyles and personalities. Most people are extremely busy, and when they finally are able to take time from their busy schedules to talk to you, they're already committed and want to do business right away. In these cases, you should accomplish several steps all at once, in a single meeting. To do this successfully, you need to be organized and ready to implement solutions immediately.

Also keep in mind that prospects will often come to you because they have stopped communicating with their old adviser. (Either the previous adviser has dropped the ball and stopped talking to the prospect, or the prospect has decided to move and has stopped contacting the old adviser.) Either way, that prospect's money is not being monitored by anyone. With the markets moving so quickly today, you need to be able to move promptly in these situations.

Get a Commitment at Every Stage

Dan Sullivan, whose *Strategic Coach* program has taught us a lot about the sales process, recommends that you constantly try to get a commitment from the prospect. These commitments can be either verbal or nominal written contracts, and can be as simple as a commitment to another meeting. The point is that you get the ball rolling from your very first contact with the prospect.

Without these sorts of commitments, you run the very real risk of doing a huge amount of work without getting any payoff. You'd be giving away everything you've learned over your career. We've found a couple of excellent ways to secure commitments from prospects, both of which work on the principle that when people exchange even a token amount of money they become much more focused and committed to what they are doing.

The first is to charge the clients up-front for a service, with the understanding that we'll adjust their fees accordingly later. For instance, we might charge an hourly or flat fee to create a financial plan, and then give them credit for that charge if they decide to work with us. Not only does this make the prospects much more serious about the process itself, it makes them much more likely to choose to become our clients.

The second way is to ask the prospect to move at least some assets to you from the very beginning. Explain to the prospect that the work you'll be doing requires a great deal of time and expertise, and that for you to commit to that work, you need a commitment in return. The amount of assets needn't be large to secure the commitment.

Leave a Take-Away at Every Step

Another suggestion from Dan Sullivan that we've found very effective is to give both prospects and clients a physical, tangible reminder of you every time you meet with them. Examples include client questionnaires, capability brochures about your organization, a summary of the data that have been gathered, an outline of the client's stated goals, and copies of signed contracts. At the point when prospects become clients (very rarely before), you can also give them a copy of the actual details of your recommendations.

Bring Your Whole Team into the Process

A great way to show prospects the value you deliver is to show off your team. Bring in different members of your staff to participate in the different elements of the process, making sure to match the personality and expertise of each person with the most appropriate element. You wouldn't want to charge your top salesperson with gathering data, for instance, or have your best bean counter responsible for client presentations.

We do this at our firm by having one person, often Cliff, initially meet with the prospects to tell them about our capabilities, what we want to accomplish, and the team they'll be working with. He asks the questions that help us understand the direction in which they want to go and that prequalify them as clients for our firm.

At that point, if we were creating a financial plan, for example, we'd bring in our planner, who's a great stickler for getting all the small details he needs to make a good plan. If we were doing money management, we'd bring in our money manager to collect the needed data and then present the investment policy statement to the client.

After all this, when we were ready to sign on the prospect, Cliff would come back and ask the prospect, "How does it all sound?" He'd then address any issues and get the firm commitment to move ahead. By operating like this, we make it clear to the clients that they're getting the services of a team of highly qualified specialists.

Making the Transition to Consulting

MANY ADVISERS we work with have converting their commission business to fees as one of their goals, and we know that for a lot of them it's not an easy goal to reach. Particularly if you have an old-fashioned client base that works strictly on a product basis, converting is going to be a major challenge.

But if your client base lends itself to consulting, your job is much easier. If you undertake this transition, we recommend that you break it down into the following four steps, which worked well for us when we converted many of our clients to fees.

1. Be Prepared

Have your consulting process largely in place before you attempt to convert anyone. You can continue to polish the fine points of the process once you've begun implementing it, but you must have all supporting elements in place in advance.

You'll also need to identify the way (or ways) that you will charge fees. These can include hourly fees, flat fees, assets under management fees, and performance-based fees, to name a few. Make sure that all of the appropriate disclosures of your fee options are made in your required regulatory documents and client documents.

In terms of compliance, keep in mind that you may be required to demonstrate to regulators that you'll be providing additional, ongoing services that will justify your fee. Also, because you initially will incur a lot of expenses by working on a fee basis, but not a lot of income, plan carefully to ensure sufficient cash flow during your transition.

2. Identify Clients You Want to Convert

Go through your client list and sort out the ones who would benefit by switching from a transactional to a consulting basis. From this list, find those with at least $100,000 in investable assets (or whatever amount you determine is the minimum with which you can work on a fee basis). Now choose from this group your best clients—the ones who trust you the most and whom you like working with the most. These clients should be the first you try to convert.

Keep in mind that your conversions need to be cost-effective. Your largest clients may not necessarily be the ones you should try to convert first. If you anticipate that a particular client will require a lot of persuasion, hand-holding, or cajoling, skip him, at least in the beginning. You'll want to refine your process with your easier clients before tackling the more difficult ones. When possible, at this time you may want to move the clients you know will never work on a fee basis to a junior adviser in your firm.

Above all else, the conversion must be in the client's best interest. If the conversion will not leave the clients in a better position for achieving their goals, don't do it.

3. Meet with the Clients You Want to Convert

Let the client know that you would like to make some changes in the way you do business in order to provide better service and be of more assistance in reaching her long-term financial goals. Briefly explain the steps of the advanced consulting process and how you charge fees, and then invite the client to come on board.

4. Implement Conversion

Assuming that the client agrees to convert, you need to undertake some fact-finding, just as in the discovery stage. If you have not met with this client recently, keep in mind that there may be substantial changes in her particular situation. Once you have this information, move ahead with the remainder of the consulting process.

CHAPTER 4 **Build High-Impact Client Relationships: A Crash Course**

I N OUR BUSINESS, relationships are everything. If you don't build strong relationships with your clients, it won't matter if you're the most brilliant investment manager in town—you still won't reach the ranks of highly successful advisers.

Conversely, if you make your relationships with clients your top priority, you'll consistently capture new opportunities in both good markets and bad. But it's not enough just to say that you focus on your clients. You need to have systems in place to ensure that you act on this focus day in and day out, year in and year out.

In this chapter, we look at each aspect of building high-impact client relationships:

- exactly what it means to be client-centered
- how these client relationships can pay off in terms of your assets under management

- how to systematically build lasting, profitable relationships

The Client-Centered Adviser

OF COURSE, probably every adviser you talk to would say that he is focused on his clients. After all, many people got into this business, at least in part, to help others. But actions speak much louder than words, and when you really look at how advisers actually work with their clients, you'll find that most fail to consistently communicate with their clients in a meaningful way.

To get some perspective on this, let's look at one study by CEG Worldwide on how advisers relate to their clients. In this study, the researchers found that advisers fall into two distinct groups: *investment-centered advisers* and *client-centered advisers.*

Investment-centered advisers tend to be most focused on making sure they have the best investment program for clients. These advisers are focused on the investment side to such an extent, in fact, that it comes at the expense of their existing clients and prospects.

Client-centered advisers, conversely, put a greater focus on their relationships with clients than they do on their investments. This is not at all to say that they are not concerned about investments or are not skilled investment advisers, but just that their clients are their top concern.

How does the different focus of each group translate into action? It turns out that these two basic orientations color nearly everything advisers do in their practices. **FIGURE 4-1** shows just how dramatic the differences are between these two kinds of advisers.

A couple of factors are especially striking. A huge major-

FIGURE 4-1

Issues Important to Advisers' Practices

Shaded rows indicate client-centered advisers' concerns

ISSUE	PERCENTAGE OF INVESTMENT-CENTERED ADVISERS WHO SAID VERY IMPORTANT	PERCENTAGE OF CLIENT-CENTERED ADVISERS WHO SAID VERY IMPORTANT
Talking to current clients	15.8%	92.9%
Analyzing the market	69.1%	14.3%
Reassuring clients	20.8%	97.6%
Strategizing about their business	61.1%	31.0%
Personally contacting prospective clients	16.8%	84.5%
Working on balancing portfolios	47.1%	7.1%
Meeting with clients	19.8%	88.1%
Analyzing client investment positions	53.4%	10.7%
Immediately responding to client inquiries	66.4%	100.0%
Strategizing about the stock market	57.4%	6.0%
Asking clients for referrals	7.3%	78.6%
Talking to their peers	76.7%	36.9%

SOURCE: CEG WORLDWIDE, LLC. *THE BEST OF TIMES*, 2001. SAMPLE SIZE: 608 ADVISERS

ity (88.1 percent) of the client-centered advisers said that meeting with clients is very important, but just 19.8 percent of investment-centered advisers stated this to be a priority. More than three-quarters—78.6 percent—of the client-centered advisers reported that asking clients for referrals is very important to them, compared to just a handful (7.3 percent) of the investment-centered advisers.

These kinds of differences would indicate that investment-centered advisers are often too busy with investment analysis (you could even say they have "analysis paralysis") to spend meaningful time with their clients.

FIGURE 4-2

Success of Investment-Centered Versus Client-Centered Advisers

ADVISER RESULTS OVER PREVIOUS SIX MONTHS	INVESTMENT-CENTERED ADVISERS	CLIENT-CENTERED ADVISERS
New clients	1.3	6.8
Average assets per new client	$51,000	$269,000
Clients providing additional assets	0.8	7.3
Average assets from current clients	$13,000	$64,000
TOTAL new assets over last six months	$76,700	$2,296,400

SOURCE: CEG WORLDWIDE, LLC. *THE BEST OF TIMES*, 2001.
SAMPLE SIZE: 608 ADVISERS

So does your primary focus make much difference in how successful you are? Absolutely. As you can see in FIGURE 4-2, client-centered advisers over the six-month study period acquired many more new clients; had many more existing clients give them assets; and ended up with much, much more in new assets.

The math is easy. Total new assets for investment-centered advisers were $76,700, but almost $2.3 million for client-centered advisers. By focusing on their client relationships, these advisers acquired almost thirty times more assets than the investment-centered advisers.

(New clients x average assets per new client)
+ (Clients providing additional assets x average assets from current clients)
= Total new assets over last six months

Investment-Centered Advisers:
$$(1.3 \times \$51,000) + (0.8 \times \$13,000) = \$76,700$$

Client-Centered Advisers:
$$(6.8 \times \$269,000) + (7.3 \times \$64,000) = \$2,296,400$$

It's important to note here that the study was conducted in April 2001—in the midst of a protracted market downturn— when many advisers would have considered themselves doing well just to stay even. There were no significant differences between the two groups in terms of years in business or the markets they served. What did make the difference is their emphasis on client relationships.

We certainly experienced a similar response in the period following September 11, 2001, when we did several things in our local firm to reach out to clients.

First, we immediately sent out a well-crafted letter to all of our clients that lent some long-term perspective to what had happened; not just what it would mean for the markets, but what it meant to all of our lives. We stated our opinion of the catastrophe's impact on the market and the prospects for long-term recovery, as well.

We also published this letter in our local newspaper on the day after September 11. The effect of this was to instantly instill the confidence of the general public in us. We had an opinion and were not afraid to communicate it, and people at that time were looking for exactly that kind of leadership. We ended up getting quite a few new clients from this—primarily clients who had lost trust in their previous adviser—as well as receiving referrals from centers of influence around our area who saw the letter and sent prospects to us.

To create some one-on-one contact with our clients after September 11, we held an open house at our office. We arranged to have a very well-respected investment strategist available by conference call during the event to give his perspective and answer questions from our clients. We got an outstanding response to the open house from our clients—they were able to gain some useful information from the conference call, but more important, it helped us make some meaningful connections and create a sense of community during a difficult time.

Finally, we held a series of monthly seminars during this period, inviting both top clients and prospects. Each seminar started with a review of what was happening in the market, along with some historical perspective. Then we made a presentation about the way changing demographics in the future will be influencing the markets, the economy, and the businesses of the clients present. We pulled in many new clients this way, as well as new assets from existing clients. The key thing that made it work was that we created a completely nonthreatening, nonmarketing environment in which people could get some useful information and see some friendly faces.

Contact Your Clients— or Someone Else Will

THE BUCK STOPS WITH YOU. If you don't step up to the plate and actively fill the role of trusted adviser to your clients, you can be sure that some other adviser will be happy to. Go on the offense. When issues arise, don't just let them fester, hoping that clients won't notice or that the issue will just go away (or even worse, don't do what we've heard some advisers do—run out the back door the second they see their clients coming in the front door). You have to stand up, provide some leadership, and reach out to your clients.

Client communication is all about being proactive. Clients need to know they are working with someone who knows what's going on, has definite opinions, and will be there when times get rough. You have to be able to make them realize that the market is not their friend, and that it will try to push them out at the worst possible time. You must make this kind of communication an absolute priority, doing it all the time and not just when you feel you have a few spare minutes.

In our local practice, we've found that the following techniques have worked the best for us over the years in helping us to build meaningful, profitable bonds with our clients.

Make Your Communications Systematic

We use a highly effective computer-based marketing system we purchased from Bill Good Marketing more than fifteen years ago that we believe is still light years ahead of off-the-shelf contact management programs. This is a complete system containing not just software, but also extensive training and guidelines on how to maximize every client contact.

The system contains all our client contact information (which was imported as part of the cost of the system), and a library of hundreds of constantly updated letters. It features complete prospecting campaigns that include a series of letters with phone call scripts, as well as "feel good" letters such as birthday letters, thank you letters, and get-well-soon letters, to name but a few. Every letter is excellent as is, but can also be edited, if we choose, before sending it to our compliance department for approval.

The system allows us to easily select which letters we want to send and when, and customizes each one with clients' names. This is far easier and faster for us than drafting letters ourselves from scratch. (Our very successful September 11 letter, for example, was provided to us by Bill Good.) The system also provides tools for tracking and reporting the results from each letter campaign.

Because this system freed us up to focus on the activities that actually make money (letter-writing is definitely not one of those activities), it easily paid for itself in the first month after we bought it.

Make Every Single Contact Personal

Every written communication to your clients should have their name and your signature on it, and be as customized to each client as possible. For example, each of our clients receives a birthday letter every year, and each letter is unique. One year, we sent a letter that described what happened during the year they were born, like major news events, who was president, and which songs were popular. Another year, we sent a letter that listed celebrities and historical figures who shared the same birthday.

It's important that you sign each card or letter personally, and not use a digitized signature. This gives you a chance to add a personalized, handwritten postscript to each letter, and also ensures that you cleanse your list, removing clients who have left you or passed away. We know some advisers who just have their systems create the signatures, but we can't think of anything more embarrassing or damaging to your credibility than having a birthday or anniversary letter with your signature on it arrive at the house of a client who has died. Taking the time to personally see and sign each letter will not only prevent this awful situation from happening, but just might jog your memory about some potential business idea that you'd like to share with the client.

Also, have a real person answer your phone. In our own business, we steadfastly refuse to ever have a client or prospect get lost in the maze of an automated answering system. We can't think of a better way to communicate to a client that we don't appreciate their business or value their relationship than to let a computer answer our phones.

Contact Clients the Way They Want to Be Contacted

A contact can be anything from an e-mail or phone message to a letter, seminar, or one-on-one client meeting. One type of contact isn't better than any other, and you can't rely on any single kind. You do need to understand how your clients want to be contacted and how often. Ask them at your very first meeting. Beyond your regular communications about their portfolios, ask if you can be in touch about other items you believe would be of interest to them, such as seminars or information about new investment vehicles and wealth management strategies.

Make Your Communications Consistent

Your clients should be able to set their clocks by when you contact them. At our firm, we have someone contact every money management client at least every ninety days (unless the client has opted for less frequent contact). We let them know that we've looked over their portfolio and whether we have any recommendations for changes. We ask them to let us know about any questions they may have, as well as any changes in their life (an inheritance, job change, or divorce, for example) that we should be aware of. All other clients also hear from us regularly through the letters we send out.

Let Them Know You Care About Them as People, Not Just as Clients

Make it a point to contact your clients about events or issues that have nothing at all to do with their portfolios, the markets, or new offerings. Drop them a note on their birthdays, send cards (or a small gift) around the Christmas holidays, and acknowledge any other events or holidays that are important to your clients. These "feel good" contacts will let them know that they can expect more from you than just sales pitches.

In our firm, we tend to focus especially on the patriotic holidays like Veteran's Day or Memorial Day. When we sent out one letter on Veteran's Day with the poem "High Flight" ("Oh! I have slipped the surly bonds of Earth...") by WWII pilot John Magee, we received an amazing flood of thank you letters from clients. Many were from World War II veterans who told us about their memories of the war and how much they appreciated our acknowledgement of them. We ended up feeling much closer to many clients for really very little effort on our part.

Events are another great way to let clients know you care. Think about throwing an annual celebration for all the clients in your firm, perhaps during the holidays. We've also seen nice success with events that all the clients can rally around, like a race or volleyball tournament to benefit a charitable organization.

Be Innovative

One of the most successful things we've ever done is to convene "family meetings" with some of our top clients. They work like this:

We reserve a room at a local private club and then invite the clients to a dinner meeting at our expense. If the clients are agreeable to letting their adult children know about their assets, we invite them and their spouses. Then we bring in the clients' accountants and attorneys, as well as our staff.

We set the agenda and control the conversation through-out the evening. In short order, we're able to gather every-one's input, get important decisions made, and give everyone specific to-do lists to accomplish what was agreed upon. In addition, if the kids have their own money that we manage or advise, we'll meet with them in breakout sessions at the end of the meeting.

Using this format, in just one evening we can accomplish a great deal:

- We get to cement the relationship and demonstrate how important the clients are to us.
- We put everyone—clients, kids, other advisers, and our-selves—all on the same team. By doing so, we end up with a better-rounded course of action and are better able to get things done.
- We create a meaningful connection between ourselves and the next generation in the family, putting us in an excellent position to receive their business in the future.
- We ensure that the grown children are aware of their parents' investment strategy and, where appropriate, have the opportunity to provide input.
- We are able to introduce our staff and have the clients get to know them. Where clients previously were willing to meet and work only with Cliff, they're now happy to meet with other members of the team.
- We have the chance to show off our capabilities and team to the attorneys and accountants. This is great from a networking standpoint, because they are centers of influence and can provide access to other potential clients.

Communicate in a Language They Can Understand

Charts and graphs will only go so far with many clients. Instead, use plain language, stories, and examples as much as possible to help make your points. We are constantly harvesting "client-friendly" ideas to be able to communicate on a basis they can easily understand.

For instance, we had a client come in one day railing about the market—which was down at the time—who insisted that he sell because he was sure that the market would never come back. We could have tried to convince him to stay in the market by telling him that 97 percent of the previous ten-year rolling periods in the market had been up, but we doubt that would have been very effective. Instead, we simplified the concept and said, "Look, you have 100 horses you can bet on. Ninety-seven of those horses have *never* lost a race. Do you really want to bet on one of the other three?" Once we explained it that way, he immediately decided to remain in the market.

Make It Easy for Clients to Respond

In every single sales-related communication, such as letters about new products or ideas, include a way for clients to quickly and easily respond to you. We do this by including a coupon at the bottom of each letter we send. The coupon has a set of boxes clients can check to let us know, among other things, if they need to discuss their portfolio immediately, if they have a referral we should contact, or if they have additional assets they'd like us to provide a second opinion on. A call to action above the coupon reads, "Clip coupon— return today." We include a business reply envelope so that the clients can easily mail it. We get these coupons back from clients all the time, and not once since we started using this system has a client said, "You never contacted me."

By the way, we've found that these kinds of letters are a terrific way to stir up interest and dialogue in a nonthreatening, low-key (or even no-key) manner. We often hear clients say, "Hey, I got your letter. I'm not quite ready to do anything right now, but I'll call you as soon as I am." Other times we use these letters just to let clients know that we can offer them particular products that they may not have known about, such as annuities, life insurance, long-term care insurance, and mortgages. We've consistently received good responses from these letters.

Proactively Communicate About Mistakes

If any kind of blunder occurs that's going to affect your clients, don't just sit back and pretend it's not there. You need to jump on the issue, clear it up, and then communicate to clients exactly what went wrong, why it went wrong, and how you're fixing it.

We had to deal with this kind of mistake recently when our clearing firm erroneously included a message with its monthly client account statements that stated our firm was no longer servicing their account. It instructed the clients to either take delivery of their securities or have another adviser move their accounts immediately. Fortunately, a member of our staff noticed the message while reviewing statements online (and while they were still in the mail from the clearing firm to the clients). We contacted the clearing firm, had it overnight a letter to every single client that explained that the message was intended for clients of another firm and that our own firm remained their servicing firm. We then did a calling campaign, having our money manager contact every client to let them know they would be receiving the two letters and to reassure them that we were most definitely still working with their accounts and that they need not be concerned about us.

Because we were so proactive about it, we turned something that had the potential to be very damaging into a nonevent. We also received some additional business as a result of the phone call campaign.

Leverage Technology

E-mail, of course, has become extremely important in how you communicate, making it much easier to get in touch with clients quickly and to respond to them immediately. But you should always be on the lookout for other tools that will help you get the most relevant information to your clients as quickly as possible.

Some advisers we know, for example, hold conference calls on a regular basis with investment strategists. They invite their clients to call in (via a local or toll-free number), they interview the strategist, and clients have the chance to ask their own questions. The conference service they use makes a recording of the call, which they then place on their website and e-mail out to key clients who may have missed the call.

Shun All Mass, Nonpersonalized Communication

We've found that any nonpersonalized communications, such as the boilerplate newsletters that you take and stick your own name on, are of zero value. They look like exactly what they are—junk mail—and often don't even reflect the true views and capabilities of the advisers who send them out. Think about it: If you were a client who had several different advisers, what would you think when you received the exact same newsletter from each adviser? What a waste of time and money!

CHAPTER 5 # Take the Wheel: Don't Let Your Business Drive You

A DVISERS THESE DAYS are stretching to get the most they possibly can out of every minute of the day. They are confronted with seemingly endless demands on their time, from remaining current on the newest investment vehicles down to the smallest detail of running their offices. In fact, a CEG Worldwide study found that a majority of advisers—60.1 percent—identified difficulty in managing their own time as a significant obstacle to success.

To succeed in this environment, you have to find ways to manage all these challenges so that you can focus on what truly delivers the value in your firm: building strong client relationships.

This means you must manage your practice as a business by finding ways to leverage your time, increase productivity, and improve client satisfaction, all while keeping an eye on the bottom line. You have to make it a priority to work *on* your business, not just *in* your business. Working harder won't get you where you want to go—you have to work smarter.

In this chapter, we focus on the three major areas of managing your practice well:

- delivering the right *services*—the ones your most profitable clients want, not simply the ones you want to offer
- using *systems and processes* that deliver these services efficiently and consistently
- employing suitable *technology* that supports your marketing efforts, service delivery, and operations and that does so at a reasonable cost

Offering the Right Services

SUCCESSFUL BUSINESSES don't just provide the services, such as retirement planning or investment management, that they like. Instead, they provide both the number and type of services their most profitable clients want. Both our experience and the research tell us that affluent clients demand a comprehensive range of services. A study done by CEG Worldwide of 778 super-affluent investors (those with at least $5 million in assets) shows that clients were dramatically happier when they were offered multiple services.

Only 15 percent of the affluent clients surveyed were sold three or more services, but an overwhelming majority of this group was satisfied—96.6 percent, in fact, reported satisfaction with their advisers. In contrast, 65 percent of the affluent clients were offered only one service. Of this group, just 39.9 percent reported being satisfied. (See **FIGURE 5-1**.)

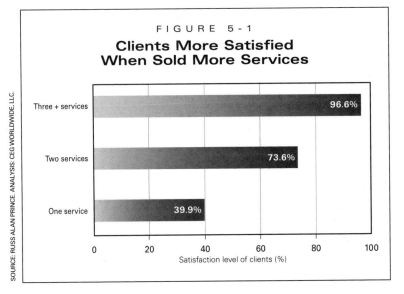

FIGURE 5-1

Clients More Satisfied
When Sold More Services

Three + services — 96.6%

Two services — 73.6%

One service — 39.9%

Satisfaction level of clients (%)

SOURCE: RUSS ALAN PRINCE. ANALYSIS: CEG WORLDWIDE, LLC.

When you offer multiple services, you create a truly win-win situation for both your clients and yourself. Your clients receive the array of services they need to meet their financial goals, and you have the chance to cross-sell, build deeper relationships with your clients, and effectively set yourself apart from your competition.

But if you are part of a small (or even mid-size) firm, how can you offer this broad range of services? We've seen some advisers individually endeavor to become experts in several different areas, none with much success. It's simply too difficult for any single adviser to gain the deep expertise that affluent clients need in more than one area.

What *does* work, however, is to focus on a single service, becoming a true expert in that specialty, and then outsource other services. We've found that offering a single service can be a very strong business model, provided that you are able to outsource services beyond your expertise,

FIGURE   5 - 2

Services Affluent Clients Want
from Their Financial Advisers

SERVICE	PERCENTAGE OF CLIENTS DESIRING SERVICE
Asset allocation	56.7%
Financial and estate planning	41.2%
Tax planning	23.5%
Manager-of-managers	1.5%
Asset protection	1.0%
Family business planning	0.8%
Philanthropic advisory	0.7%
Education/information	0.2%
Advice/counseling	0.1%

SOURCE: RUSS ALAN PRINCE AND KAREN MARU FILE, *CULTIVATING THE AFFLUENT (INSTITUTIONAL INVESTOR,* 1995). ANALYSIS: CEG WORLDWIDE, LLC. SAMPLE SIZE: 879 AFFLUENT INVESTORS

either to formal strategic partners or to an informal network of other providers.

We've seen many advisers expand their services outside of traditional financial planning through such partnerships or networks. For example, they're now able to offer (or refer) tax preparation and planning, mortgages, insurance, and trust services. Not only are they better able to meet the needs of more sophisticated clients, they can more easily differentiate themselves from their competitors. (We go into much greater depth on creating these kinds of successful partnerships and networks in Chapter 7, "Building a Deeper Bench: Forge Strategic Alliances.")

Obviously, you can't simply increase the number of services you offer and expect this to draw in clients. You also need to carefully align your service offering with the interests of the clients you want to attract and retain.

SOURCE: RUSS ALAN PRINCE AND DARLENE DEREMER, *MARKETING MUTUAL FUNDS THROUGH INDEPENDENT ADVISERS*, 2001. ANALYSIS: CEG WORLDWIDE, LLC. NO SAMPLE SIZE AVAILABLE

FIGURE 5-3

Affluent Private Clients' Interests Are Changing

PRODUCT	PERCENTAGE OF CLIENTS WHO HAVE PRODUCT	PERCENTAGE OF CLIENTS INTERESTED IN PRODUCT
Private equity funds	0.0%	42.2%
Fund of funds	0.6%	32.2%
Hedge funds	3.0%	55.9%
Managed accounts	27.4%	38.0%
Variable annuities	17.0%	13.0%
Unit investment trusts	9.7%	5.8%
Exchange traded funds	17.0%	35.0%
Mutual funds	52.0%	5.5%

A survey of affluent investors pinpoints the services that they are most interested in. As FIGURE 5-2 shows, a majority (56.7 percent) wanted help with asset allocation, followed by 41.2 percent looking for financial and estate planning. Tax planning followed a distant third, and a grab bag of other services was named by only a tiny percentage of survey respondents.

Your own perspective may be different, so use your in-depth knowledge of your target market to guide you in your selection of services. Also, look at what is being offered by those who traditionally serve that market.

Next, go deeper and identify the specific products you might offer. For purposes of discussion, let's look at the most common one: mutual funds. Another study by CEG Worldwide (FIGURE 5-3) shows that client interests are changing, and that the investments most commonly offered are not necessarily the ones that they have the most interest in.

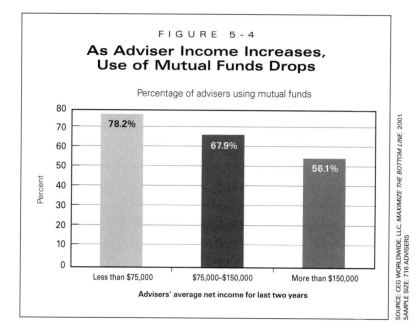

FIGURE 5-4

As Adviser Income Increases, Use of Mutual Funds Drops

Percentage of advisers using mutual funds

SOURCE: CEG WORLDWIDE, LLC. *MAXIMIZE THE BOTTOM LINE.* 2001.
SAMPLE SIZE: 716 ADVISERS

In no instance is the gap between what clients have and what they really want larger than in mutual funds. Although more than half of the affluent investors surveyed (52.0 percent) own mutual funds, a mere 5.5 percent are actually interested in them going forward.

If you assumed from this that the advisers who are selling a lot of mutual funds are not the most successful advisers, you'd be right. FIGURE 5-4 clearly shows that as adviser income goes up, use of mutual funds drops. Nearly four out of five (78.2 percent) advisers earning less than $75,000 offered mutual funds, whereas slightly over half (56.1 percent) of advisers making more than $150,000 did so.

Those results are completely in sync with our own experience in working with more sophisticated advisers. They believe they can add value well beyond what is gained through simply investing in mutual funds. In addition, when selling to their more affluent investors, they see little reason to pitch a brand name mutual fund that these clients could buy anywhere, including from most other advisers, online brokerages, or directly from the fund company. Going even further, some of these advisers believe that offering an investment product that has largely been commoditized would actually, in their clients' perception, decrease the value they offer.

Our aim here is not to slight mutual funds. In fact, their use is entirely appropriate in many cases. We often rely on funds to accomplish important objectives, including:

- investing in areas outside of our expertise, including foreign investing and certain sectors.
- obtaining a particular product selection, such as a group of preferred bonds.
- investing for moderate-income clients who need the diversification mutual funds can offer.
- achieving proper asset allocations in institutional accounts.

Rather, our message is to not blindly follow the crowd when choosing what range of options to offer your affluent clients. Don't assume that just because a particular vehicle is popular with the investing public in general that it is necessarily right for your affluent clients. As we've seen before, offering only products that have largely become commodities will not add substantial value to wealthy investors.

To help your decision-making process, we suggest that you answer the following questions about any new potential service or product:

- Will it increase my ability to attract and retain affluent clients?
- Will it meet the specific needs of my target market?

- Will it allow me to effectively demonstrate to my clients and prospects the value I can add to their financial lives?
- Is this offering a commodity—one that clients and prospects could obtain anywhere—or is this a unique offering that meets a unique need and requires specialized knowledge?
- Will it increase my net income and generally support the financial success of my practice?

Building Efficient, Effective Systems

GREAT SYSTEMS ARE the cornerstone of a successful advisory business. They provide your clients with a seamless, enjoyable experience; make your employees as productive as they can possibly be; and build tangible value in your business. Without reliable systems, your drive to make your firm a success will be uphill all the way.

Perhaps the best way to illustrate the impact of good systems is by way of an example. Let's take preparation for client meetings. One adviser we know created a detailed checklist of about twenty-five actions that must be taken before every client meeting. He put the procedures for using the checklist in writing, and his staff has been trained to ensure that everyone completes the tasks in the same way, every time.

Among other things, the checklist calls for the portfolio report to be prepared in a very specific way, with returns and maturity dates reported in a defined manner. In addition, it requires all client notes since the previous meeting to be printed out so that the adviser can familiarize himself with any changes that have taken place in the client's portfolio or personal situation. This keeps him completely updated on what has happened, even if he was not involved. Once the checklist is complete, one person is responsible for double-checking each item to ensure that it was done correctly.

This one simple tool helps this adviser accomplish some of the most important tasks in running a practice:

Guarantee a consistent client experience. All clients enjoy the same high level of service, every single time they meet with the adviser. Clients are comfortable because they know what to expect and can count on the process unfolding the same way each time. We've found that whenever clients experience this kind of consistent service, they tend to make more referrals. They know that their friends and associates will have the same dependable level of service, so they feel much more comfortable referring them. In contrast, we've seen inadequate service cause clients to leave much more often than investment performance does.

Operate efficiently. When procedures are clearly defined and communicated to employees, it ensures that they are doing precisely (and only) the work that is required. By using a procedure that is always done in the same way, regardless of which staff person is doing it, training is easier and disruptions from staff turnover are minimized. Because the system is thoroughly documented, it becomes relatively easy to modify as needed to either improve it or adapt it to changing circumstances.

Ensure accuracy. It's much easier and less costly to do things right the first time than to go back and try to correct an error. Especially in our industry, small mistakes can quickly become big problems, getting the adviser in trouble both with clients and compliance.

Put the focus on the entire team, not just one star player. When an advisory business is sharply focused on the adviser, every client wants (and expects) to see only the adviser. This leaves advisers with few ways to leverage their time or employees. By creating systems that provide a consistent experience, clients become more willing to meet with others in the firm. In any efficiently run company, the service team is likely to have more client contact than the advisers.

Create equity in the firm. Too many advisory firms are overly reliant on the adviser, with all systems dependent on him or her to function properly. It's nearly impossible to build significant equity in a practice when all value creation lies with a single person. But with systems in place that allow others to sustain and replicate business, even without the adviser's presence, equity is built in the systems themselves.

Systems like these don't just happen. They require that you think of your business functionally, constantly looking at your procedures for ways to improve. Taken as a whole, the following set of techniques will give you an excellent start in developing effective systems in your own practice.

Focus on the results you want. Don't be so overly concerned with the few errors you might be making that you forget to define exactly what you want to achieve. The first step you should take in building effective operations is to envision and describe how you would like your business to run. Take the time to put this vision in writing. This will be helpful both to ensure that you remain on track as you develop your systems and to benchmark your progress.

Review the client experience. Starting with the new account process and continuing every time you have contact with your clients, you have an opportunity either to impress clients or lose them. Look at every aspect of your clients' experience as it is now, identifying every instance where any facet of the experience is less than top-quality or inconsistent from one contact to the next.

No detail of the client experience is too small. Don't overlook things such as the appearance of paperwork sent to them, or how they are greeted when they call on the phone or have an appointment in your office. Don't have trade journals sitting out on the coffee tables in your client waiting area. Likewise, don't have consumer magazines (such as *Sports Illustrated*) on your own desk when you meet with clients. Don't offer your clients coffee in paper cups. At our own firm we serve it in china, or mugs imprinted with our company logo that they can take home.

Create an organizational chart. Who does what and when? Who manages workflow to ensure that you meet established standards? Who is in charge of what, and who answers to whom? Draw up an organizational chart and job descriptions, even if you are the one who initially fills most of the positions. Use it to identify gaps and redundancies.

Clearly distinguish between sales and service. Your sales team and service team should be completely separate so that each can focus on and succeed at its tasks. We've found that unless the two functions are kept firmly delineated, the service work (which does not generate additional revenue) will always be done before the sales work (which does).

Hire the right people for the right jobs. Recognize that some people are naturally inclined toward sales, whereas others never will be. Likewise, some people excel at and enjoy client service, whereas others do not. If you hire a born salesperson to do service work, he simply won't succeed, regardless of how hard he works. We use a number of different tools to match people to jobs, including the exercises developed by Dan Sullivan's *Strategic Coach* program, as well as a test developed by the Kolbe Corporation that helps identify people's natural tendencies. (See Resources for more information.) We have also used outside consultants to interview and hire candidates, keeping us out of this time-consuming process until final approval for the hire is needed.

Include self-checking mechanisms. Clients trust you with their life savings. If you can't provide an acceptable performance statement on a timely basis, they will naturally question your competency in other areas—as well they should. Identify where mistakes are likely to be made by opening an account for yourself and walking through the process from A to Z, and then put means into place that will save you from the common mistakes such as missing signatures or blanks not filled in.

Document everything. Write down the procedures that work and update the documentation each time you make an improvement. Go systematically, noting all the details. Repeatable procedures can develop out of individualized solutions that work—if you have taken the time to note what works. Your goal should be to create a business blueprint or a detailed description of your firm that includes both the "big picture" of operations as well as the fine points.

Involve employees. Your employees bring their own perspectives about how the business can run more smoothly and will perhaps be your most valuable source of ideas for systematically increasing productivity. Soliciting their feedback will not only draw out their ideas, it will also give them a stake in the systems that are created in response to their ideas.

Examine how you spend your time. It's easy to be extremely busy, but still not spend your time on the activities that produce the greatest rewards. As the Pareto Principle says, 20 percent of time expended tends to produce 80 percent of the results. Your goal should be to spend as much time as possible on the items that will show up on your paycheck stub and minimize the time you spend on everything else. **Keep a time log for a few days to understand exactly where your time is going.** Split out how much time you spend on every activity, from opening your mail and returning phone calls to client meetings and prospecting. If your experience in tracking your time is anything like ours, you'll be surprised at how little time you actually spend where it really counts—with your clients, generating revenue.

Step into your clients' shoes. A single thing should underpin every decision you make about which systems to employ: What is most important to your clients. Your clients care little about your systems. What they *do* care about is working with a trusted adviser who can help them reach their financial goals. Don't get so caught up in constructing efficient systems that you stray from the primary reason you're in business—satisfying your clients' financial needs.

Get outside help. Finally, we've seen many advisers benefit in this area by using consultants specializing in system and process development, human resources, and cost control. It can also be extremely valuable to find out how other advisers are handling similar issues, so consider joining a peer study group. There are also a number of highly effective professional coaches and coaching programs specializing in financial practitioners or entrepreneurs. (We talk more about how to get this kind of coaching help in the next chapter.)

Leveraging Technology

AS YOU SAW in Chapter 1, "Five Trends, Endless Opportunities," technology has never been more important to advisers than it is today, and this importance will only continue to grow over time. Although technology has gone far toward increasing productivity and client service, it can cost you more in time and money than it saves if you don't manage it well.

The challenge is to harness technology so that it serves you, and not the other way around. In our work with advisers, we've found the following three steps to be key in getting the most from information systems.

Know What's Out There

Capabilities are constantly expanding, but you should stay as current as possible on what technology can do for you. Leave no stone unturned—you don't want to miss out on potentially valuable and profitable tools.

These are the most important functions that now rely heavily on technology:

Client presentations. Many prospects and clients are coming to expect advisers to illustrate their ideas and approaches with multimedia and even interactive presentations.

Client communication. From e-mail to robust websites, technology has transformed the way most advisers communicate and offers all advisers important tools for building stronger client relationships.

Marketing and branding. Customers now routinely expect every business to have a Web presence, and a well-designed and regularly updated website helps a firm to build its brand and credibility with clients and prospects.

Account aggregation. Consolidating the accounts held by a client with one firm is now easy, but pulling together the information from each one of a client's accounts, including those not under the management of the adviser, remains difficult.

Order entry. Web-based order entry and routing systems give advisers the ability to trade quickly and easily place trades.

Client account viewing. These online systems allow clients to see their account information, including positions, balances, activity, and trade confirmations, as well as 1099 statements.

Portfolio evaluation. These programs track every detail about a portfolio, including history, positions, tax basis, and real-time returns, and can provide hypothetical tools that allow advisers to test strategies and simulate the results.

Stock and fund research and evaluation. Because of the sheer volume of research data available online the primary challenge is now to filter out the noise and identify the most up-to-date, comprehensive, and user-friendly sources of information.

Financial planning, estate planning, and insurance planning. Planning software can generate plans relatively easily and quickly, but are limited by the built-in assumptions that are used to derive the results.

Electronic document storage and retrieval. By converting paper documents to digital records using scanners and optical character recognition systems, much less time and money is being spent on filing and storage. Electronic document storage also helps facilitate the increasing mobility of advisers.

Bookkeeping. A range of high-quality business bookkeeping programs exists to handle payroll, taxes, and accounts receivable and payable. For fee-based advisers, client billing systems that calculate and process the collection of advisory fees have also been developed.

Time management. A number of scheduling and project management tools are now available, many integrating, with varying levels of success, with other programs. We can't imagine running our business without Palm and Microsoft Outlook technology.

Contact management. Contact management systems have made it easier for advisers to step up their customer service and more easily maintain their client relationships by organizing client information and automating certain communications, such as birthday or holiday greetings. The best systems are extremely versatile, letting you cross-reference and access information in many different ways.

Marketing and practice management information. The Internet holds a wealth of data on target market groups, client newsletter templates, turnkey seminar programs, practice valuation guidance, and information on how best to run your office, to name just a few.

Regulatory updates. The Internet makes it easy to stay abreast of changing regulations and requirements, with the NASD making regulatory updates available on its website and by e-mail subscription.

Compliance. Technology has eased the compliance headache, making it much easier to oversee the work of others to ensure proper compliance and reporting.

Mobile links. An assortment of technologies, from cell phones to personal digital assistants to programs that allow remote access to the office network, has given advisers the flexibility to work from nearly any location with a phone and an Internet connection.

Continuing education. Advisers are now able to fulfill many of their CE requirements online through both self-study and interactive courses offered by a number of different educational organizations.

Marketing and coaching systems. There are now systems that enable advisers to design marketing and business development strategies and then help implement them by providing benchmarks, task lists, and project management assistance.

Use Your Technology People Wisely

Tools are only as effective as the people using them. The following will help you benefit as much as possible from the tech wizards who make your systems tick.

Have a dedicated technology person. As a broker-dealer, we love to see advisers who have a staff person devoted solely to technology issues. A dedicated tech person is a common denominator of successful advisers because of the huge increase in productivity and decrease in costs that this one person can bring. One adviser we work with has told us that hiring a tech person has freed up ten hours per week of her own time. Given a firm with two service assistants, one tech person can easily replace one assistant and double the productivity of the other. When hiring a tech person, look for someone with knowledge and experience in networking systems and programming. Because he or she will serve as the internal company "help desk," the tech person should also possess excellent people skills.

Make your tech hires carefully and deliberately. Instead of hiring new tech people outright, work with them on a consulting basis before making any commitments. You might have them work on a single, specific project, without giving them access to your entire system, to see how they work and how they fit with the rest of your team. Remember that the skills they bring to the job are much different from your own skills and those of other people on the staff. This makes communication more challenging—it's easier to misread and misunderstand them, and harder to connect in a meaningful way.

Help your technology person network with others. Just like you need to interact with people who do similar work, so do tech people. Because often they are the only tech person in the office, it's easy for them to feel lonely and isolated in their jobs. There are plenty of opportunities for you to help them out with this. If you're at a conference, for example, and meet an adviser who has solved a particular technology challenge, get the name and number of her tech person, set up a call, and introduce that tech person to your own. You can help them get a conversation started around that particular issue, but more often you'll find that they'll carry on the connection beyond that initial phone call. In our case, we've helped hook up the technology people in our advisers' offices with the tech people at their vendors and our clearing firms so that they've been able to develop peer groups. They can share solutions, keep current on the latest technology, bounce ideas off one another, and generally get the support of others in similar situations.

Be prepared for when your technology person moves on. Although it's important to have a Plan B for replacing any staff member, it's critical to think ahead about the possibility of losing your technology person. Know local contractors, outsource vendors, and the technology people at your broker-dealer so that at a minimum you'll be able to keep functioning if your tech person leaves on a moment's notice. Go out of your way to know the people at your neighborhood PC repair shops and in the tech departments of your local high schools on a first-name basis. All of these people will be a huge resource for you if you need to make a replacement.

Get to know the technology people at your broker-dealer, your clearing firm, and vendors that you work with. These folks can make a huge difference in how much time and energy you end up spending on technology, so a little effort in creating great relationships with them will go a long way. Be aware that they speak a language that's often impossible for nontech people to comprehend. It's especially helpful to introduce your own tech people to these contacts—because they speak the language, they can help translate.

Choose Your Products Carefully

All programs are most definitely not created equal. These guidelines will help you avoid wasting your time and money on products that don't pay their own way.

Critically evaluate the resources you devote to technology. We see many advisers make the mistake of assuming that all the money spent on technology is necessarily well spent, and others just spend too much altogether. Technology seems to be the last place they put cost controls into place. Before you commit to any new technology purchases, run thorough cost-benefit analyses.

Watch it work in the real world. Don't simply take the word of salespeople about the marvels of any new technology, and don't assume that hardware and software will work in your office the way it does in a vendor's demo. When possible, visit other advisers, preferably along with your tech person, who are currently using the product to see it in operation. We've found that most advisers are more than willing to do this (and you, in turn, should make yourself available to others for the same reason). If you can't visit in person, contact them by phone. Any vendor should be willing to give you references to other advisers who are using their products. If they are not, be wary. Always attempt to negotiate with the vendor to get a free trial period of sixty to ninety days to ensure that it really is a product you need and will use effectively.

Be skeptical. Don't assume that the latest and greatest application is necessarily going to work before you buy it, and understand where it may not be compatible. For example, we work with an adviser who needed to install new trading software in order to work with the clearing firm. The adviser had just upgraded to Windows 2000 (which he needed to run other programs), but the clearing firm could only assure the adviser that its software would work on Windows 97!

Also, plan on multiplying the conversion or ramp-up time given to you by a vendor by a factor of two or three.

Don't reinvent the wheel. We've seen advisers go to enormous effort and expense to create custom systems that were essentially their own versions of software that is already widely available. Remember, you're in the advisory business, not the technology development business. Chances are good there are applications available off the shelf that will meet your needs—take advantage of them.

Volunteer to beta test products. When the vendors and clearing firms have new programs and systems that they would like to roll out, they often look for volunteers to try them out in advance of their release. When there is a particular product that is critical to your business, this can be extremely valuable. You'll have a real voice in how it is developed, and ultimately it will work better for your particular situation.

Get the best price. We've found that many technology companies are very hungry and willing to negotiate their prices in ways that you might not even imagine. If you're looking at two similar products, for example, you can always ask one manufacturer to match the price of the competing one.

Get help. Make sure that the technology you select is not so far ahead of the curve that you end up getting burned. We like the phrase "leading edge—not bleeding edge" to describe our technology. Keep in mind that the regulators or your compliance department may also have a say in which tech tools you employ. Most recently, the Monte Carlo simulation software has come under scrutiny, and certainly websites and chat rooms continue to be a hot regulatory topic. This is a great area to seek outside help, going to experts in a particular technology (and its associated rules and regulations) who can give you excellent advice.

Don't wait to start. Many advisers hold off on making any investment in technology, determined to wait just a little longer for the latest and greatest version of software or hardware. The problem is that there will never be any "final" product—technology will continue to develop at the same rapid pace in the future as it has in the past. Technology will only become more complex, so the longer you wait to take the technology plunge, the steeper your learning curve will be once you do. Progress won't wait for you to get your feet wet—make the leap now.

CHAPTER 6 # $E = MC^2$, or Education $= $ More Compensation^2: Commit to Ongoing Learning

T O SUCCEED IN OUR BUSINESS, you need every single edge you can possibly get. We've found that ongoing education is one of the key things that separate the truly successful advisers from the less successful ones. We're not just talking about racking up your required CE credits, but rather committing your money and time to an active, deliberate educational program, both for yourself and for your clients.

In this chapter, we look at how to get the most from your educational efforts, including:

- how education matters to your bottom line.
- which areas you should focus on and the most effective ways to accomplish your learning.
- how you should be educating your clients.

Education Pays

IN OUR OWN CAREERS, education has made a tremendous difference in what both of us have been able to achieve. It has been a continual source of information, ideas, and tools that we've been able to put to use to help not just our broker-dealer, but also the advisers who work with us and the clients in our local practice. The coaching program in which we participate has been especially helpful in getting us to set goals and follow through on achieving them. Without it, we would not be at the level we are today, and we would be stuck in many of our old habits.

The research tells us that we're not alone in this positive opinion of the value of education. One CEG Worldwide study finds that there's a gulf between how the top-earning advisers see education and how the lowest-earning advisers view it. When they were asked about the kinds of help

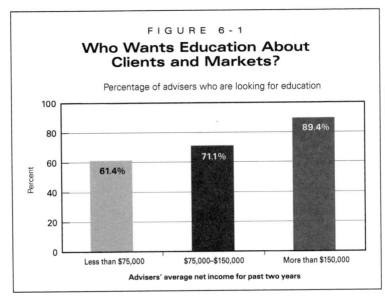

FIGURE 6-1

Who Wants Education About Clients and Markets?

Percentage of advisers who are looking for education

SOURCE: CEG WORLDWIDE, LLC, *MAXIMIZE THE BOTTOM LINE,* 2001.
SAMPLE SIZE: 716 ADVISERS

they were looking for from financial institutions, nearly 90 percent (89.4 percent) of the most successful advisers said education about clients and markets. This compares to just 61.4 percent of advisers earning less than $75,000 per year. (See FIGURE 6-1.)

It's important to understand that it's not just your own education that you need to be concerned about. As we discussed later in this chapter, the investment you make in your clients' education can pay for itself repeatedly in client satisfaction, client retention, and new clients.

Educating Yourself

THE EDUCATIONAL opportunities out there are nearly limitless, but they each offer something different. To get anything of real value out of them, you need to carefully target where you spend your time and money.

There are two educational tracks: the technical issues track and the business development track. The technical issues track covers subjects like the newest product, recently introduced technology, or the latest tax law. The business development track, conversely, helps you work *on* your business, not just *in* it. It challenges you to take an honest look at how you work now and structural changes that will let you work more efficiently and profitably.

One track is not better than the other; you have to go down both. We see too many advisers spending their time only on the technical issues track. It's much harder to find good business development support and practice management information, but if you want to take your business to a higher level, you'll need to locate these resources and commit to getting the most from them.

So how do you leverage your limited time and money for

the most educational benefit? Two baseline questions will help you focus your efforts:

What business do I want to be in? This will tell you which *subjects* you need to educate yourself about. To answer this question, you must have a clear idea of what you want your business to look like: the clients it serves, the services it offers, and how it is structured.

Who are the top people who can help me in that business? This will tell you which *people* (or which types of experts) you should access in your educational activities. Your answer will affect every decision you make related to your education, including which seminars you attend (and how you spend your time at those seminars), who you choose for a coach, or what kind of study group you take part in.

Seminars and Workshops

You want to look for the events that provide information in your target subject areas, of course, but look at the opportunities they give you to connect with others just as carefully.

For us the major reason for attending any seminar or conference is less the subject matter and more the networking opportunities. The presentations are generally educational, sometimes entertaining, and usually take care of CE requirements, but the real value for us is found in the hallways, exhibit halls, and at after-hours events. (We even know some quite successful advisers, in fact, who spend *all* of their time at seminars networking and skip the presentations altogether.)

To contact specific people who can be of help to your business, go to the presentations and breakouts that address the subject matter most important to you. Connect with the presenters afterwards, ask for their cards, and ask if you can follow up if you have questions later. (You can save a lot of money in consulting fees by doing this.) Network with the people you're sitting with during these sessions— they might introduce you to their own network. Be a good listener, but don't just suck up ideas from others. Actively give and take and share your own ideas.

A terrific workshop that combines both of these elements for us is held each year by our friend Bill Good (see Resources for details). We never miss this event for two reasons:

It delivers leading edge trends and practices. Bill is very skilled at identifying trends and giving broad insights into where the business is going. At the same time, he is also very good at pinpointing specific techniques that can make all the difference in the world in the operational efficiency of an adviser's office. He discusses the latest technologies available to advisers, how to interact with staff, how to compensate staff, and how to set up your office.

It brings the top people in the industry together. He brings in highly successful advisers from all types of firms who share details on everything from how they work with clients to how they operate their offices to how they conduct their seminars. It's very valuable to see where the rubber meets the road—participants don't just get ideas, they see how these ideas are actually implemented in the real world. This is also extremely valuable to us from a networking standpoint, because it allows us to hook up with other industry leaders.

Another conference that we've found to be particularly useful is the Financial Planning Association's annual convention. Because it attracts exhibitors from every part of the industry—mutual fund companies, clearing firms, broker-dealers, variable annuity providers, life insurance companies, and technology vendors, to name just a few—

it provides an excellent overview of the trends in products and services. Because it's one of the best-attended conferences in our industry, it allows us to network with large numbers of advisers, especially financial planners.

Other good events that combine useful information with good networking are the seminars that are held by product manufacturers such as mutual funds companies and insurance companies. (These events are quite often by invitation only to the top producers.) Because they are offering the same products as you, other advisers like yourself attend these events, giving you the chance to brainstorm around challenges you both face. These seminars also give you the opportunity to network with top people at the product vendor. When you later experience any kind of problem, it's great to be able to phone up the head of marketing or head of underwriting directly.

We've found that clearing firm conferences (such as those held by Schwab, TD Waterhouse, and Pershing for their advisers) are another good educational resource. Because the specific technologies and services offered by your clearing firm can change so rapidly, there is often no better way to keep up—even your marketing contact may not know everything that is happening in your clearing firm.

Coaching

If you choose to get help from a coach or coaching program—something we highly recommend—your choice of coaches should again be guided by the two questions: "What business do I want to be in?" and "Who are the top people who can help me in that business?"

There are many, many coaches available who can work with you one-on-one. Some are focused on helping people with general life goals and direction, whereas others specialize in a particular area. For example, there are coaches to help you be a better financial adviser, or coaches who will help you become a big life insurance producer. Some coaches specialize even further, helping you with a very specific aspect of your business. If you choose to work with a coach individually, the best way to locate a coach who would be a good match is through networking and getting referrals.

There are also a number of group coaching programs out there, including ones conducted by well-known industry figures like Steve Moeller, Dan Sullivan, Bill Bachrach, and John Bowen. These programs tend to be focused on business development, helping you to see what you're doing now and how you can do it better. Some target a particular aspect of your business. Bill Bachrach, for instance, offers a coaching program designed to help you perfect your client interview skills.

Working with a good coach or coaching program will help you look at your business from a completely new angle. It will make you take the time you need to really think through what is most important to you and how to achieve it. It will require you to define exactly the best type of client for your business. It will force you to plan, something most people completely neglect to do. And it will help you each step of the way as you move toward your goals.

We participate in a group coaching program offered by Dan Sullivan, entitled *Strategic Coach,* which we've found incredibly valuable. It provides a framework for you to decide for yourself, "What is my unique ability? What do I want to do? What do I love to do? What am I passionate about? How do I do more of what I love to do and less of all the things I dislike doing?"

Once you're clear about this, it then takes you, step by step, through building a team that will allow you to do more of what you love (and truly excel in) and less of what you hate (and do poorly). Then it takes you through a process to decide what the unique benefit is that you bring your clients. It helps you nail down exactly what is unusual and valuable about your practice—something a lot of people have a very hard time doing—so that you can communicate that effectively to prospects.

A big part of coaching has to do with time re-engineering. This isn't time management, which is just finding ways to be more efficient with your time, but rather taking a close look at how you really spend your time. Too many advisers lose themselves in busy work, like doing client service work, returning e-mails, and dealing with their mail. This prevents them from doing what they are supposed to be doing to make their businesses a true success: selling and meeting with clients.

Our coaching program meets once every quarter for an entire day, with no distractions. This gives us four days out of the year to do nothing but think through our lives, our businesses, and what we want to accomplish. Many times before these meetings we've found ourselves saying, "We just can't take this time out." But we've made the time every single quarter, and it has turned out to be the best possible use of our time because we are so much more productive and focused on what we want to accomplish.

Don't underestimate the incredible impact of taking some time off on a regular basis to think about your business and where you want to go. One amazing thing we've experienced in our coaching program is the power of goal setting. We spend part of our day every quarter listing all the items we want to accomplish over the next three months. Being very busy, we usually don't refer back to the list until the next quarterly meeting. When that meeting rolls around and we take another look at it, however, we find that nine times out of ten we have reached every goal we set. The very act of verbalizing your goals, discussing them with others, and writing them down is enough to drill those goals into your mind and set everything into motion to achieve them.

This program has helped bring about serious changes in the way we do business. When Jill joined the firm in 1993, Cliff had his hands in every aspect of running the day-to-day operations of the business—every staff person reported directly to him, he was solely responsible for all management duties, and he took care of all HR functions. These kinds of jobs were simply not the best use of his skills. He was unhappy with the situation—no one is happy doing things they're not good at—but he was reluctant to let it go.

It took the coaching program for him to give up those things. It made him realize that he was better at doing other things, and that one of Jill's strengths was her ability to build a team that could take over those day-to-day duties. With her team in place, he could really focus on his passion and expertise—strategic thinking and partnering—and begin firing on all cylinders.

Study Groups

Study groups can be quite valuable, provided you find the right group. The very best study groups are well organized, have clear missions and agendas, keep all their members active, and frequently bring in outside presenters.

The most common way for advisers to hook up with study groups is to be invited directly by a member of an existing group. This kind of invitation will come from the networks you've established with other advisers and other professionals throughout the industry. You can also get involved with a study group through your local chapters of professional organizations to which you belong, such as the Financial Planning Association or life underwriter groups. Another alternative is to start your own group, inviting in associates you feel would be good sources of new ideas and inspiration.

Help from Product Wholesalers

Wholesalers, or the business development managers who represent financial institutions and work with financial advisers, can be another important source of assistance. There is a huge amount of pressure on wholesalers today to provide real value and educational ideas that advisers can implement immediately. We've seen some advisers tell their wholesalers flat out, "Unless you're bringing me a good idea that I can put to work right away, don't bother coming in."

Many product sponsors are responding to this pressure, and as a result there is more and more good help out there available from wholesalers, if you know what to look for. At a bare minimum, wholesalers you choose to work with should be able to give you the following:

Product knowledge. All wholesalers are going to know the intricacies of their own offerings, but the valuable ones will provide tools to give your clients some perspective on the market in relation to what they are selling.

Marketing and sales assistance. Besides turnkey marketing processes, they should offer you ways to give a different twist on a product to generate new interest. Some wholesalers may be able to provide you with the names of prequalified leads. We've found that one of the most effective ways to use wholesalers is to request that they give us a presentation on their products, as if we ourselves were clients. This can really help you to sell to your own clients in turn.

Some wholesalers will offer to present seminars for your clients themselves. We strongly suggest that you never let wholesalers make presentations without seeing them yourself first—there is simply no other way for you to know if they are good presenters than to see for yourself. Better yet, have them give you the tools for an outstanding presentation. After all, you want clients to bond with you, not the wholesaler, and you are the one who needs to be seen as the expert in the eyes of your clients.

Practice management support. They should be a continual source of ideas on improving your operations, as well as information on the best practices of other advisers. Some of the best wholesalers will bring in top speakers on practice management for you to earn CE credit. Other top wholesalers can be your coach, mentoring you on many different aspects of running your business well.

Educating Your Clients

THERE IS A LOT OF GOLD just waiting for you in your client file cabinet. One of the best ways we know to get at it is by continually educating your clients. Just like the wholesalers who come to you need to bring along new ideas or tools, you need to have useful information and ideas to offer your clients that will add genuine value.

Some advisers offer general financial planning or investing basics seminars that revolve around their need to sell certain products. This won't cut it. People are looking for help, so you need to focus on their specific needs. You want

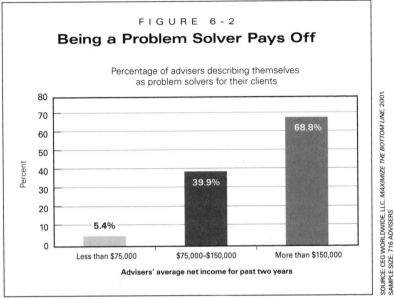

FIGURE 6-2

Being a Problem Solver Pays Off

Percentage of advisers describing themselves
as problem solvers for their clients

SOURCE: CEG WORLDWIDE, LLC, *MAXIMIZE THE BOTTOM LINE*, 2001.
SAMPLE SIZE: 716 ADVISERS

to position yourself as a problem solver for your clients—
someone who can give them exactly the information and
perspective they require to meet their financial challenges.

The research tells us that advisers have plenty to gain
by investing time and money in their clients' educations
in order to be seen as this kind of problem solver. As you
can see in **FIGURE 6-2**, more than two-thirds of advisers earning more than $150,000 per year described themselves
as problem solvers for their clients. But just a few—
5.4 percent—of the advisers making less than $75,000 saw
themselves this way.

You have two major opportunities for educating clients:
in one-on-one settings, such as client meetings and
phone calls, and in group settings, primarily seminars
and workshops.

One-on-One Education

These are the major areas where you need to be prepared to offer your clients information and education:

Your perspective on their investments. We often hear from clients, "The stock market has never acted like this before. It's different this time, so I've got to act now." More often than not, though, it *has* acted that way before, and there's good reason to believe that it probably will again someday. By helping your clients to step back and see what has happened in the past and why things are happening now, you'll calm their fears and help them set reasonable expectations for their investments. Many will also want your perspective on the overall economy, politics, and current events, and how all those factors affect their portfolio.

The background on your recommendations. Give them the "whys" behind your recommendations, looking at their goals, time horizon, and risk tolerance. Also, let them know what trends you see happening in the future that may affect their holdings.

The mechanics of their investments. This includes items like how mutual fund expenses and loads affect the value of their fund investments, and how fund values are calculated. Don't assume that your clients know the basics—we've come across new clients, for example, who believe that "no-load" means "no cost." We once almost lost a client because he believed that the value of his mutual fund investment had not grown in years. He looked only at the share price (which had not gone up), and failed to take into account that the number of shares he owned had increased dramatically.

Specific investment or financial planning topics. As changes occur in your clients' lives, like a new baby, a divorce, or retirement, fully explain the solutions that may now be appropriate for them. Educate them on how the related financial products would work, their advantages and disadvantages, and alternatives.

General life planning issues. Many clients come to us looking for some direction and problem solving around life goals. When it's appropriate, we'll provide some tools and exercises, which are drawn primarily from our experience with coaching.

Group Seminars

Seminars are an excellent way to educate your clients on key topics, but also help you to build your client relationships and pull in prospects. Over years of designing and fine-tuning our seminars, we've found the following to be the most important steps in creating a perfect seminar:

Target the right message to the right audience. It's important that you fully define your audience and its needs in advance so that you can provide content that fits. Find topics that are pertinent, timely, and useful. We've conducted seminars in the past on subjects ranging from 529 plans and tax-free income to estate planning and long-term care insurance. Depending on the topic, you can develop your own content, use a turnkey program designed for the affluent (such as those available from Harry Dent; see Resources), or use content offered by wholesalers.

Follow a focused agenda. It's very, very important to know exactly what you want to achieve and to have an established process and agenda for how you are going to proceed. The content will vary according to your topic and goals, but every seminar you conduct should include these elements:

- a presentation of your firm's capabilities and team
- a description of what the audience will gain from the seminar

- a presentation of useful information targeted carefully to attendees
- a commercial that suggests what the participants can do next and why they should do it with your firm
- a Q&A period to allow you to respond to questions or concerns
- a closing that briefly repeats the commercial and conveys your gratitude to the audience for attending

Rehearse thoroughly. Practice your presentation so you don't fumble around or miss important points. Rehearse it in front of a colleague who can point out areas where you can improve. If you need to, script the entire presentation to ensure that you use the best words and phrasing for the points you want to make.

Keep it small. We've found that the smaller the group, the better. This lets you make your message more customized and focused directly on the individuals in the group. When our seminar audiences have included prospects, we tend to close nearly every single prospect when the group consists of ten or fewer attendees. With larger groups— like twenty-five—we have a much lower close rate.

Get the clients there that you want. Send letters to people you believe would be interested in a specific seminar. To really make sure that you get the clients there that you definitely want, though, you'll need to call them. (It will be the call that gets them there, not the letter.) Stress during the call exactly how the seminar will be of benefit to them. In light of the recently passed "do not call" rules, be sure that you follow your firm's procedures on making these calls.

Have the right tools ready. Put all your presentation materials into professional-looking binders or folders for attendees. Use catchy visual aids (such as PowerPoint presentations or overheads) whenever possible, and make sure in advance that they're working properly. Always use round tables so that people can easily talk with one another.

Make it entertaining. Don't let your audience get bored. Mix up the pace and break up the session into short, digestible sections. Use plenty of audio and visual effects in all your presentation materials. Be creative and make it fun.

Invite clients to bring their friends. There's no better way to draw in qualified prospects. A great idea we have heard is to ask clients to be "table hosts" for seminars. Tell them there will be three couples at each table, so they can invite two other couples who they think would enjoy the seminar. People really respond very well to this—it gives them a chance to invite their friends to dinner and spend some time with them. As a prospecting tool, it's perfect: you get someone else out there prospecting for you and giving the prospects positive testimonials.

Encourage questions. Taking questions is one of the most important things you can do, because it makes attendees feel that the seminar is all about them. If you're worried that clients won't have any questions for your Q&A period, you can plant a question in advance with someone in the audience you know well. This will get additional questions rolling. We've also handed out silver dollars to people who ask questions, which, understandably, has always drawn a good response.

Get feedback. Always prepare an evaluation form for your seminar guests to fill out and hand in before they leave. This form allows your audience to tell you what's working, what's confusing, and—most important—what follow-up they would like from you. We encourage the audience by giving out a small thank you gift in exchange for their completed forms. We always have a simple gift that relates to something enjoyable from the presentation and that includes our name and phone number on it. And we always have the gift wrapped, as it just adds something special to the effect. Don't skip this step, because this is when many prospects will turn into clients.

Don't bother advertising. Putting an ad in your local newspaper to announce your next seminar and invite the general public is a great way to tell your competitors exactly what you are doing and to have a bunch of people show up who are just interested in a free lunch or dinner. You need to target your audience and invite them directly.

Fine-Tuning Your Client Education Skills

We've known a number of very successful advisers who were teachers in previous careers, and we don't think this is just a coincidence. The skills you learn through any kind of teaching, training, or public speaking will all be extremely useful when it comes to educating your clients effectively, so we strongly suggest you seek out this kind of experience. Toastmasters is a great organization for cultivating your public speaking skills (see Resources).

Cliff has been a longtime active supporter of Junior Achievement—the national organization dedicated to teaching kids about business—because he sees it as a great way to help children. But it's also been a way for many people in our local firm to get some great public speaking experience. By volunteering to teach in the classroom for Junior Achievement, they've learned how to hold the audience's interest, how to keep a presentation moving along and hitting on the key topics, and how to overcome their nervousness about speaking in front of groups. If you can keep the interest of eighth graders, you can keep anyone's interest, and all of our advisers who have gone through this program have become excellent presenters.

CHAPTER 7 **Building a Deeper Bench: Forge Strategic Alliances**

T HE FINAL KEY STRATEGY for your success is to build strategic alliances with other professional advisers, specifically accountants and attorneys. These kinds of strategic alliances are the single most powerful way we know to build your business and serve your clients better. In one package, they connect you with new, prequalified clients; enable you to provide better all-around service to those clients without being distracted from your core competencies; and maximize your time and efforts.

But strategic alliances are not simple or easy to create. You need to cultivate them over time, building the trust and structure you need for everyone to work together effectively. CEG Worldwide's research shows that strategic alliances are difficult for most advisers, but that the top-earning advisers tend to see them as less of a challenge. (See **FIGURE 7-1**.) We would venture to say that the ability of

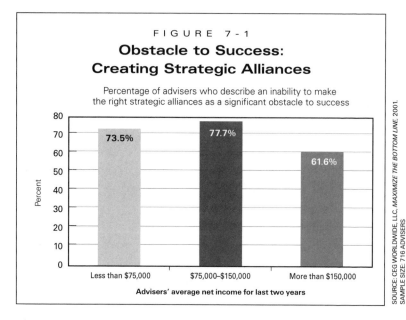

FIGURE 7-1

Obstacle to Success: Creating Strategic Alliances

Percentage of advisers who describe an inability to make the right strategic alliances as a significant obstacle to success

Advisers' average net income for last two years

SOURCE: CEG WORLDWIDE, LLC, *MAXIMIZE THE BOTTOM LINE*, 2001.
SAMPLE SIZE: 716 ADVISERS

these advisers to build alliances has a great deal to do with their success.

In this chapter, we'll look at:

- what makes every successful strategic alliance tick.
- how to cultivate referral partnerships.
- how to initiate and structure formal alliances.

The Heart of Every Good Alliance

THERE ARE THREE things that every alliance absolutely must have. Each of these is like glue: If you have them, the alliance will probably stick together and succeed; if you don't, the alliance doesn't have a chance.

Your Clients' Best Interests Must Be the Top Priority

If bringing in new business is your only reason for building a strategic alliance, it won't succeed. A good alliance *will* bring in plenty of new business to you, but it will only last and succeed over the long run if you first have your clients' interests at heart.

A common interest by everyone in the alliance on what is best for the clients is part of the bond that holds the alliance together. Everyone must be on each client's team, almost like employees of the client. If you don't have this bond, and everyone views the alliance as just a means to the end of bringing in new revenue, it will eventually fall apart.

There Must Be Trust and Respect Between Alliance Partners

You'll trust your best clients to your alliance partners, so you need to have complete faith in them as individuals and total respect for their work. Your partners must share your high level of commitment to client service, integrity, and professionalism. The last thing you want is to put yourself in the uncomfortable position of having someone send you clients whom you do not feel comfortable making referrals to in return (if, for instance, you didn't care for the quality of their work).

You also need a personal rapport. You and your partners should be a good match in terms of your personalities and your firms' cultures so that you have a common ground for building the relationship. Ideally, you might also belong to some of the same social groups.

Partners Must Understand One Another's Skills, Abilities, and Personalities

For the alliance to run efficiently, each partner has to thoroughly understand what the other partners bring to the table in terms of what they can do for the client. You should fit well with each other in your knowledge and resources, which should be complementary and compatible, and not redundant or competitive.

You and your partners should share a philosophical approach about the best types of products to offer and how best to work with clients. At the same time, keep in mind that you'll be especially successful if the ideas you bring to your alliance partners are unique. You should really know your partners as people, because it's just as important to match up the personalities you'll be working with as it is to match up your skills.

Building Referral Partnerships

THE FIRST LEVEL of strategic alliances is the referral partnership. This is a relationship between two professionals who know one another well, have similar clients, and are confident in one another's abilities to do excellent work. These partners don't refer one another in order to receive some kind of compensation, but to enhance their long-term relationships with all the parties involved.

Bear in mind that we're not talking here about a casual referral to an attorney or accountant that you happened to have met once or twice. Rather, these are referral relationships that you deliberately seek out, cultivate, and troubleshoot. Several of the top advisers in the country we know make it their top priority to build relationships with well-respected centers of influence. As a result, they receive every single one of their new clients through referrals. In our local practice, it has always been our most powerful way of getting clients, with about 80 percent of all our new clients coming in by referral.

To make this kind of referral partnership work, though,

you need to follow a few cardinal rules, all of which revolve around relationships and communication.

Know Your Referral Partners—Inside and Out

To avoid ending up with egg on your face by making a bad referral, make sure you really know your referral partners—their style, their unique abilities, and the type of clients they are looking for. Make sure that they know you, too. There's not much worse than having a referral partner send you prospects who are not qualified for your practice. This puts you in a very uncomfortable position—not only do you have to turn the referred client down, you jeopardize your relationship with the referral partner.

When introduced to potential new partners, we always look into their backgrounds thoroughly before committing to work with them. This is important: Any problems that clients may have with a referral partner will reflect directly back on you. Don't be afraid to ask around—including talking to competitors and centers of influence—to ensure that the potential partner has an excellent reputation.

We will often get to know our referral partners through working with them jointly on a client, or working with them on our own personal accounting or legal matters. It has also helped when we get involved with the same organizations as our referral partners. For example, an attorney who Cliff has worked with on estate projects is involved in a gourmet dining and wine group. At the attorney's urging, Cliff also joined the group. Besides getting to know one another even better, they've been able to talk up each other's strengths to other members of the group, which has resulted in business for both of them. But don't join a social group strictly for business. It has to be something you enjoy, with people you like, or you won't have any fun and will dislike going. In the end, you won't do your business any good.

Once you get to know someone, you have to keep up the relationship. If you don't pay attention, it could change in ways you might not expect. For instance, we once worked jointly with a tax adviser on some of our clients. It was a good experience, and he asked us to send him referrals. We did make a few referrals until one of these clients came back to us and said, "I know you referred me to him, but I don't think he's really your friend."

It turns out that this tax adviser had become allied with another financial adviser and had started referring our clients to him! We had failed to keep tabs on the relationship, and if our client hadn't been bold enough to tell us what was happening, it would have continued.

Match Horses to Courses

Being able to match the right client with the right referral partner is the key to making the long-term relationship work. You want people to work well together, so match personalities and cultures. You want them to respect each other, so look for the qualities, credentials, and experience that each will value.

Every time you refer a client, your referral partner has to follow up, enter the client into her system, possibly inconvenience herself in terms of rearranging her schedule, and finally meet with the client. If it's not a good fit, it will have been a waste of everyone's time. You can bet that the next time you call, your referral partner won't be nearly so anxious to talk to you.

It's better to give no referral than to give a bad one, so if you don't know someone who is a good match, don't make the referral at all. Tell the client that you don't know anyone who can meet their particular needs, and make some suggestions of other advisers.

If you match clients with referral partners well, you'll earn a reputation for doing so among other professionals. They'll welcome your referrals because they'll know, even before they meet them, that the clients are right for them. If you make bad matches, conversely, you'll make everyone uncomfortable—the client, the referral partner, and yourself. You'll end up being known as someone who makes everyone just spin their wheels.

Smooth the Way for Every Relationship

Whenever you give a referral, set up both the client and your referral partner for a good experience. First, tell the client that you will contact the other professional to let him know to expect a call, to explain the client's situation to him (in strictest confidence, of course), and to find out if there are any potential conflicts in the two of them working together.

Second, always call the referral partner to let him know that you have referred someone to him. This professional courtesy accomplishes several important things:

- It gives him time to prepare for the call from the client.
- It helps him to make sure he doesn't accidentally miss an opportunity by not taking the call.
- It lets him know that you are only making referrals that make sense for his business.
- It keeps your name in his mind, making it more likely that referrals will come back in your direction.

Communicate Constantly with Referral Partners

There are always inherent risks whenever you're in the business of getting people together. In most cases, though, you can sidestep many pitfalls by keeping in close touch with your referral partners about specific clients.

If a client you receive through a referral does or says something completely unexpected, check with your referral partner about it. She should be able to explain it and give you some context.

Likewise, whenever you encounter any kind of difficulty with a particular client, go back to the referral partner for her take on the situation. We once received a referral for a client who, as it turned out, traveled constantly and was extremely hard to reach. We tried multiple times to contact the prospect, but finally gave up. Later we heard back from our referral partner, who was a bit indignant that we'd never called his client. Once he told us how much the client traveled, we realized we could have prevented the problem by telling our partner about our difficulty in contacting the prospect. We now always ask about the best contact method, whether it be phone, e-mail, or letter.

Do Right by Your Referral Partners

Your referral partners need to know when the people they refer to you are unsatisfied with them in any way so that they can correct it. Occasionally when we meet with a prospect sent to us by a referral partner, the first thing the prospect does is ask us for a referral to someone in the same business as our referral partner. When this happens, we won't even touch the question.

Instead, we ask the prospect in a respectful way about the problem that is prompting the request for a referral. Then we'll call the referral partner to explain what happened. We'll share what the client's needs are and suggest that the referral partner get in touch with the client. This can be a touchy area, so be sure you spin it right so that no one ends up getting offended.

Above all, don't bite the hand that feeds you. If an accountant sends you a client, for instance, don't turn around and sabotage the relationship by suggesting that the client find a new accountant.

We once made a referral to an attorney who, because he was busy, handed the prospect off to another attorney in his office. That attorney immediately referred the client to a financial planner with whom he had his own referral partnership. The planner proceeded to try to talk the client out of working with us, wrongly criticizing every investment strategy we had in place. Obviously, it created a huge number of problems. Even though the original attorney was not directly responsible, his firm has never received another referral from us.

Building Formal Alliances

YOU CAN TAKE your strategic alliances to a higher, more profitable level by building a formal alliance. Unlike referral partnerships, which do not involve an exchange of money, a formal alliance adds "economic glue" to the relationship. Such an alliance can significantly leverage your practice by opening doors and creating new business opportunities for both you and your strategic partners.

There is a huge market of professionals out there who need your help and with whom you can create lucrative alliances. These professionals include, most prominently, attorneys and accountants. CEG Worldwide's research points in particular to a very high interest on the part of CPAs in offering their clients financial services.

Consider these key findings from a 2002 study of CPAs. Relatively few CPAs now offer investment services to their clients—just 17.4 percent. However, there's likely to be a dramatic jump in this number in the near future. In CEG Worldwide's study, nearly half of all CPAs surveyed (48.9 percent) stated that they plan to provide investments by 2005. In our own experience, we're also hearing a great deal of increased interest from attorneys in this area.

How will they do this? CPAs and other professional advisers, such as attorneys, have three primary options for making financial services a part of their practices:

Build. The CPA or attorney brings financial services expertise in-house by hiring one or more financial advisers and building from scratch all the mechanisms to deliver financial services. This could even include the firm starting its own broker-dealer.

Buy. The CPA or attorney buys a financial services firm outright, typically an RIA firm or a branch office of a broker-dealer.

Formal alliance. The CPA or attorney, together with a financial adviser, creates a formal equity- or revenue-sharing joint venture. Alternately, it can be a referral program, where the CPA or attorney provides clients to financial advisers on a case-by-case basis for predetermined compensation.

Each option obviously requires very different levels of effort and commitment and carries different kinds of risk and regulatory involvement. Which model a CPA or law firm chooses will have a lot to do with its size, resources, and ability to expand its infrastructure. Larger firms, in particular, are more inclined to go with one of the first two options.

But the good news for financial advisers is that many other CPA and legal firms are turning to the third option and looking at alliances with financial advisers. Most of the CPAs who now offer or plan to offer investments consider

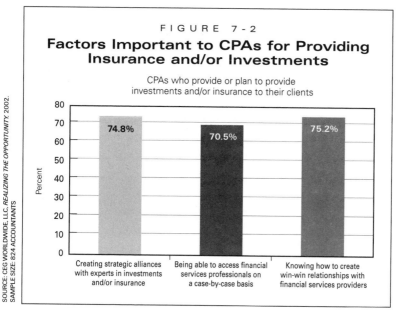

FIGURE 7-2

Factors Important to CPAs for Providing Insurance and/or Investments

CPAs who provide or plan to provide investments and/or insurance to their clients

help from financial advisers as critical to their success. As you can see in **FIGURE 7-2**, about three-quarters of all the CPAs surveyed are counting on financial advisers for help. This means the opportunities are wide open for you.

A formal alliance between you and an accountant or attorney is a real win-win situation for everyone. By offering financial services through an alliance with you, the accountant or attorney gets to add additional value to clients' lives, bring in more revenue, and differentiate from the competition. By being part of such an alliance, you get substantial new business, and get it in a very cost-effective way. The clients benefit most of all—as they must in any successful alliance—by receiving more comprehensive services and specialized expertise.

There are several specific steps we suggest you use to help build a synergistic and mutually beneficial strategic alliance with an accountant or attorney.

Target One Type of Professional

As you've seen, it's important to match your own work style and culture with that of any potential partner. As you choose between attorneys and accountants, keep these differences in mind:

- In our experience, CPAs in general are substantially less comfortable selling and marketing their services than are attorneys. This might leave the lion's share of the marketing in the alliance up to you.
- There is less overlap between the skills and allowable activities of attorneys and financial advisers. Each can do things that the other clearly cannot, leading to less concern that one will "steal" the other's clients. This can make it easier to build trust with an attorney.
- More often you'll work with an attorney on one-time events, like creating trusts or estate plans, in contrast to accountants, whose business will be recurring. This may make it more challenging to build substantial ongoing business with an attorney.

If you decide you'd like to work with accountants, bear in mind that they, among all professional advisers, guard their position as the client's trusted adviser and advocate most closely. In our work with accountants, we've found them to be very fee-sensitive and inclined to stay away from flashy, Cadillac products. We've seen their eyes light up, for example, when we've recommended tax-advantaged solutions that offer a cost-savings benefit over a traditional choice. Because it's important to them to have been seen as having made the best possible recommendations to their clients, many of them see commission-based products as tainting their objectivity.

Target One Type of Firm

You have a wide range of choices of the kind of CPA or law firm to target, from huge national firms to the one-person practice down the block. For the most part, though, it doesn't make a lot of sense to target the big firms. You'll end up frustrated by their inability to move quickly and their fear of deviating from their standard course of business. They tend to have the same approach to marketing as doctors: just wait for the phone to ring and for people to make appointments.

Instead, we've found that small, entrepreneurial-style firms work much, much better. These firms are run by people who tend to understand prospecting, are always looking for new marketing ideas, and are able to respond quickly to new opportunities. Many times they have an excellent rapport with their clients, having built their trust over many years. They can see the value of collaboration and won't automatically view you as competition.

In particular, we've seen and experienced a lot of success when both sides work in one specialty, but without a lot of overlap. Financial advisers and attorneys who both specialize in estate planning, for example, can mesh very well together.

In another case, we know a CPA with expertise in a very specialized planning niche involving insurance that requires a sophisticated knowledge of tax law. As a CPA, he had the knowledge of tax law he needed, but not the securities or insurance licenses to sell the product. So he enlisted two financial advisers to help. Now they are supremely positioned in their market—no other advisers can come close to offering that unique combination of expertise in that area.

Once you have a clear idea of the kind of firm you'll target, formulate a list of potential candidates. Ask associates for suggestions. Make note of those who get the press in your area—people frequently quoted in the local newspapers are usually the movers and shakers in the region. Ask your top clients which attorneys or accountants they use. Also, check your local business journal for lists of the top firms in your area. In all cases, you want to look for strong, highly respected CPAs or attorneys who share your target market.

Get Your Foot in the Door

By far the best route for initiating the relationship with a potential alliance partner is to be introduced by a mutual contact. Check with your networks to see if there is anyone who knows people at the firms you have targeted. This will open the door for you, begin to build trust, and help you be presold to the firm.

Lacking a network connection, cold calls are more difficult, but can still be done successfully if you position yourself in the right way. Contact influential partners in your targeted CPA or law firms to set up appointments to discuss joint opportunities. Tell them that you are exploring strategic alliances, that you share their market, and that you are interviewing three or four firms.

By saying that you are looking for a true strategic alliance—a mutually beneficial partnership designed to exploit marketing opportunities and cemented by a revenue share—you'll set yourself apart from all the financial advisers who have called them just seeking referrals. When they sense that you are offering business development opportunities, they'll put on their "marketing hat" for your interview, and try to sell themselves to you in return.

Establish a Connection

It's important from the first meeting to establish yourself as a true partner who can help the other professionals to profitably offer financial services to their clients. Clearly communicate the many benefits an alliance can bring them:

- help in building their position as their clients' trusted adviser, by expanding the areas in which they advise clients
- help with attracting and keeping clients, by giving clients more of the services they need
- help in beating their competition, by offering services their competitors do not
- help in reaching new markets, by giving them access to clients they would not otherwise reach

Let them know that you understand their major concerns about working with a financial adviser, including liability. Stress that you are interested only in forming a partnership that ultimately benefits the client the most.

Explore ideas with them. Have they ever worked with a financial adviser before? Was it successful? What were their best and worst experiences in working with a financial adviser? What are they doing now or planning to do to generate new revenue? Would they be interested in exploring other opportunities with you?

Assuming that the potential partner shares your enthusiasm and appears to be a good match, move on to the next step. If not, thank him for his time and move on.

Agree on a Plan

Together with your partner, spell out and document exactly what the alliance will look like and how it will operate. You should agree on the answers to these essential questions:

What will the alliance accomplish? Set specific revenue or additional asset goals for the partnership to achieve over an initial time frame, such as twelve months.

How will you work together? Assuming you decide to work jointly on at least some clients, clarify the mechanics of how you will do so. Which processes will be used? How will client meetings be handled—will both partners be present for all meetings, or will some be one on one? How will compliance and licensing be handled? How will expenses be shared?

What type of client will you target? If you'll be sharing revenue, smaller clients are probably not appropriate for the alliance. Decide on a particular account minimum or other threshold to filter out clients who you would not be able to serve together profitably.

How will compensation work? There are very stringent rules about the ways that fees and/or commissions can be shared, and these rules vary from state to state. In addition, the other partner might need NASD, insurance, and/or RIA licenses just to share revenue. Check with your broker-dealer, state society of CPAs, or state bar association for information on the rules in your area. Make sure you are completely clear on what is legally allowed so that you can structure the alliance properly. Stay out of any gray areas—they have a way of turning black on you.

How will the alliance market itself? Will you undertake joint marketing efforts, such as seminars? If so, what are the responsibilities of each partner?

Get a Commitment

It's not at all unusual for different partners within a firm to initially fail to agree on (or even effectively communicate about) a proposed strategic plan. For this reason, you should talk to other members of your partner's firm (including, most important, the firm's managing partner) to gauge their level of commitment to the alliance. Address and satisfy any concerns they present to you.

Finally, put the alliance through this litmus test: If your strategic partner is willing to give you her own account to manage, as well as her top clients' money, the partnership is a go. If she is not willing to do so, walk away from the deal. You have to have that degree of trust or the alliance simply will not work.

PART 3

Mission Possible
Maximizing Your Broker-Dealer Relationship

We believe that the one primary relationship that can make the most difference in your business—either positive or negative—is your broker-dealer affiliation. The right broker-dealer can support all your efforts around all the strategies we've discussed so far. The wrong broker-dealer, conversely, can divert your focus and impede your progress.

In this section, we give you a framework that will help you understand whether you're now with the best broker-dealer for your practice, and provide some perspective on your major alternatives, should you decide to change. We show you exactly what to look for when you're evaluating broker-dealers, in order to choose the one best matched to you and your business, and explain how to take care of the details to ensure a smooth transition to a new broker-dealer. If you're currently with a wire house, bank, or insurance company, we also look closely at the advantages and disadvantages of going independent, and how to do so. Finally, we show you how to get the greatest possible benefit from your partnership with your broker-dealer.

CHAPTER 8

The Search for Greener Pastures: Your Independent Broker-Dealer Choices

C HANGING BROKER-DEALERS is never easy, so you want to first be absolutely sure that you really do need to make a change in order to achieve your business goals. To do so, you have to take a close look at where you want to go and how your broker-dealer is helping you (or failing to help you) get there.

Then if you do decide to switch, you need to know that your new broker-dealer is actually going to be able to support you in the direction you want to go and will not just present you with a different set of problems. For this, you should take a good look at all your options—there may be some you've never considered—to get a good understanding of what each can offer you.

In this chapter, we cover:
● the decision to make a change.

- your four major choices of independent broker-dealer types.
- advantages and disadvantages of each.

Is a Change Right for You?

IF YOU'RE CONSIDERING switching to a new broker-dealer, you have plenty of company. A study by CEG Worldwide of all three major adviser segments (independent representatives, stockbrokers with wire houses, and Registered Investment Advisers) finds considerable interest among advisers in changing their broker-dealer. Independent representatives in particular—more than four in ten— think it's likely they'll change. (See **FIGURE 8-1**.)

But is a change right for you? It's always easy to assume that the grass is greener someplace else, but to actually make a sound decision you need to take a hard look at

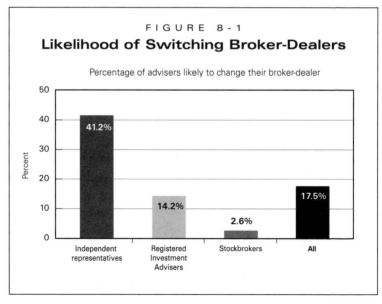

FIGURE 8-1
Likelihood of Switching Broker-Dealers

Percentage of advisers likely to change their broker-dealer

SOURCE: CEG WORLDWIDE, LLC. *THE FUTURE OF THE BUSINESS*, 2002.
SAMPLE SIZE: 1,117 ADVISERS

specifics and objectively compare apples to apples.

If you're a top producer—or on track to becoming one—broker-dealers are competing for your business just as hard as you're competing with other advisers for affluent clients. Just as you have to stand out from the crowd by offering the outstanding service and niche products these investors demand, the broker-dealers must also differentiate themselves.

It's not enough for them to just offer basic clearing, compliance, and support services. To attract the advisers they want to work with most, many broker-dealers are offering a wide range of other assistance, including in-depth training, turnkey marketing processes, and sophisticated technology platforms. Others compete for your business by providing specialized products or extremely personalized service. Still others offer their advisers a high degree of autonomy and flexibility.

There is no "best" independent broker-dealer; there is only the best choice for you. To narrow down your choices, you need first to have a clear understanding of where your business is today, where you'd like to take it, and the kind of help you need from a broker-dealer to get there. We recommend that you ask yourself the following questions to create a framework for your decision. Give these questions some thought, and write down your answers.

Where is my business today? Note specific benchmarks, including your net income, gross revenue, assets under management, number of accounts, and average account size. Assess the value you deliver clients, including products, service, communication, and education. Evaluate your marketing efforts and results, including referrals from clients and other advisers. Look at employee efficiency, satisfaction, and turnover. Include how your business affects your personal life—does it consume all your time, or is it part of a high-quality life for both you and your family?

Where do I want to go with my business? Next, consider where you want to take your business. Using the benchmarks from the first question, set short-term (twelve months) and long-term (three to five years) goals. Be very specific about what you want to achieve. Also, look at any other "big picture" issues. Maybe you would like to open an additional office in a new geographical location, build a practice that you can leave to your children someday, attract new partners, or transition your firm to new owners.

How can a broker-dealer help? What kinds of support do you need to build your dream practice? Are there specific products you need to serve your target market? Do you need the brand name of a well-known broker-dealer to market effectively, or do you want the ability to brand yourself? What kinds of technology do you need? How much flexibility do you need from your broker-dealer to operate and market as you like?

By doing this exercise, you should arrive at a very good idea of whether switching broker-dealers is right for you. If your current broker-dealer is providing what you need to move toward your goals, you're probably just fine where you are. But if there are gaping holes that will prevent you from moving forward, a change may be in order.

If you're currently working for a wire house, bank, or insurance company, you may be considering going independent. As you well know, this is a big change, which you should weigh very carefully. We look in-depth at this question in Chapter 11, "Look Before You Leave: Going Independent."

If you're already an independent representative, your next step is to decide which type of broker-dealer is right for you. You have four major options: starting your own broker-dealer, joining a large broker-dealer, joining a small broker-dealer, and dropping your licenses altogether and setting up shop as an RIA. To help you decide, we'll look next at the pros and cons of each.

The Four Options

Starting Your Own Broker-Dealer

We know that many advisers dream about starting their own broker-dealer. These are the reasons we hear most often:

- to get the complete control over their business that they would only get from having their own broker-dealer
- to have the flexibility to do what they want, when they want to do it
- to keep 100 percent of their payout
- to escape from a particular management structure or their branch manager
- to be able to offer an extremely specialized product or service (for instance, to sell viaticals or use a particular investing strategy) that no other broker-dealer will touch
- to experience the pride that goes along with saying, "I own my own broker-dealer"

That is the dream. Unfortunately, many advisers who start down the road toward opening their own broker-dealer don't really appreciate what it takes. It's important to understand both the start-up costs and the ongoing requirements of running a broker-dealer in order to accurately weigh them against the benefits of having your own broker-dealer.

Let's consider start-up costs first. Invariably, as in any

business start-up, these will be much higher than you antici-pate. For starters, your clearing firm deposit can easily be $100,000. You will have net capital requirements, which can range from $5,000 to $250,000, and also be required to maintain excess net capital over and above that amount. You are likely to incur considerable consulting expenses, and will need to invest significant time and money for a securities lawyer to properly construct your supervisory procedures and secure state and NASD registration. You will also need to have liquidity enough to see you through at least the first six months or so of business.

Second, you'll need to be aware of some of the ongoing requirements of running a broker-dealer. Many people overlook errors and omissions insurance, for example, whose premiums skyrocketed with the bear market starting in 2000. The cost for fidelity bond insurance is often also overlooked. Another major challenge is the ever-growing complexity of the regulatory environment. There has been a tidal wave of new legislation in recent years that has resulted in a myriad of new regulations and requirements, and it's only going to get more complicated in the future.

Other ongoing costs you may not anticipate include accountants' fees for auditing and certifying your financial statements, additional employee costs to cover new back-office functions, and, perhaps most important of all, the opportunity cost of diverting your efforts away from your core skills as a financial adviser.

In the end, there are really two bottom-line questions that will tell you if starting a broker-dealer is the right option for you:

What is your passion? Where do you really want to focus—do you want to spend your time helping clients achieve their financial dreams, or do you want to spend it handling operations and regulatory and compliance issues for your broker-dealer?

Is it worth it financially? Is the amount of money you currently give up to your broker-dealer really worth the risk, money, time, systems, liability, and loss of focus that it would take to run your own broker-dealer? Do the math: If you are currently a $1,000,000 producer, the difference between a 90 percent–plus payout and a 100 percent payout may not be enough to make running your own broker-dealer worthwhile.

Joining a Large Broker-Dealer

Your second option is to join a large, national broker-dealer. These firms have well-known brand names, thousands of advisers, and extended infrastructures. No two are exactly alike in what they offer and how they work with advisers, but we can make some broad generalizations about the ups and downs of going with this type of broker-dealer.

In terms of advantages, these large firms generally offer a wide range of resources geared to meeting the needs of a large number of advisers, including:

Product selection. Generally speaking, large broker-dealers offer a comprehensive product selection, though many do further specialize in particular areas. A broker-dealer might specialize in supporting insurance producers, for example, if a large insurance firm owns the company.

Transitioning services. Most larger broker-dealers have transition teams in place that specialize in helping advisers smoothly depart their old firm and join the new one.

Training. Some of the larger broker-dealers have excellent training programs, which are a particularly good benefit for people learning the business. Because they serve large numbers of advisers—some just getting started and others with a great deal of experience—they generally offer training on many levels.

Community and networking. Large broker-dealers can offer excellent networking opportunities with many other advisers whose business is similar to your own and who share your market.

Marketing support. Many large broker-dealers offer turn-key marketing assistance for advisers, such as prepackaged seminars and proposals.

Technology. With their deep pockets, large broker-dealers can develop and offer some very good technology to their advisers. The applicability of it to your business and the price, however, may vary from broker-dealer to broker-dealer.

Benefits. Some big broker-dealers offer deferred compensation packages for their advisers, something their large size enables them to easily do. This kind of "golden handcuff" can be quite important to some advisers.

Financial strength. Often owned by some of the largest financial conglomerates in the world, these large broker-dealers are not likely to go out of business anytime soon.

Cash incentives to join. Some of the large broker-dealers will offer up-front money in the form of a forgivable loan or promissory note in order to attract top advisers to their firms. Advisers receiving these payments typically use them to help build out their businesses or to cover the costs of transitioning to the new broker-dealer. (Bear in mind, however, that this money usually has a commitment attached that requires the adviser to remain with the broker-dealer for a set period of time.)

Along with the advantages of their large size come significant drawbacks:

Service designed for the masses. When broker-dealers serve thousands of advisers, their infrastructure has to be geared toward supporting the lowest common denominator—the least productive, least efficient advisers who have issues that frequently require attention from the broker-dealer.

Lack of flexibility. Advisers working with large broker-dealers are largely restricted to working within the established lines. If advisers have a special situation or want to do something out of the norm (having their own RIA independent of their broker-dealer, or trying a new product with select clients, for instance), it can be difficult for some large broker-dealers to allow it. Were they to do so, it could set a precedent that requires them to make special exceptions constantly—something that a large company just can't do and still maintain their economies of scale.

Branding difficulty. Large broker-dealers are often interested in branding themselves, and their advisers may be required to support that identity, not build their own. If you were to leave the broker-dealer and had promoted yourself using its brand, it would become more of a burden to move to a new broker-dealer. (Of course, depending on your situation, you may see this not as a drawback, but as an advantage. If you're just starting in business, you might prefer to hang your hat on a big name.)

Merger hangovers. With the consolidation occurring in the industry, your company name, your business card, and your broker-dealer structure might change every time there's a merger. The people at the top may change, and along with them the entire philosophy and culture of the company.

The short story is that the larger broker-dealers provide huge pools of resources for advisers. As with any big company, however, their sheer size precludes personalized, flexible attention. When considering large broker-dealers as an option, you'll have to decide if their depth and breadth is important enough to you and your business to trade off your autonomy and agility.

Joining a Small Broker-Dealer

Smaller broker-dealers are in many ways the flip side of large broker-dealers. The strengths of the large broker-dealers tend to be the weaknesses of small broker-dealers, and where large broker-dealers fall short, small broker-dealers can excel.

What's right for you will again depend on your particular needs, but you should be aware of these general advantages and disadvantages of the smaller broker-dealers. The following are the most significant positive aspects:

Flexibility. Smaller broker-dealers have the flexibility and adaptability to handle niche businesses, allowing advisers a level of independence that is impossible at a large broker-dealer.

More responsive service. Small broker-dealers are generally known for offering a high level of personalized service, resolving problems fast and right the first time. Smaller broker-dealers may be able to offer quicker compliance turnaround, making marketing campaigns easier.

Personalized attention. There are no ivory towers at a small broker-dealer. Advisers know who's who at the firm and can generally get through to the necessary parties to get things done. The top people at the broker-dealer are also likely to be accessible and can be a valuable source of advice and ideas.

Branding. Because advisers with smaller broker-dealers are not competing with the parent brand, they may be free to build their own business brand and identity.

Adviser involvement. Advisers at smaller broker-dealers have many more opportunities to provide input and shape the offerings and direction of the company than do large broker-dealer advisers. Some small broker-dealers also offer equity ownership and stock option opportunities.

Alongside the positives, these negatives tend to be found with smaller broker-dealers:

Variable product selection. Some small broker-dealers offer complete product lines, but others, limited in their knowledge to a few areas, may be less comprehensive. Still others have specialized offerings that can fit quite nicely with niche markets.

Variable financial strength. Although it's fairly safe to assume the financial strength of the large broker-dealers, the smaller broker-dealers don't generally enjoy the same deep pockets. Many are perfectly sound, but it is an issue that you would want to visit with any small broker-dealer that you consider. The best way to do this is to request a copy of their audited financial statements, which broker-dealers are required to have. Also, you may want to ask to see the financial statements of the broker-dealer's principal owner(s) as part of your due diligence process.

Technology. Offering deep and broad technology services is more of a challenge for smaller broker-dealers, both from a personnel standpoint and a financial standpoint.

Training. In general, training will be less than the fully developed soup-to-nuts marketing programs of large broker-dealers that are designed to train large forces of people. However, many small broker-dealers are able to target training to their niche and use outside educational providers who are specialists in their niche. Examples of these niches include financial planning, estate planning, and various types of insurance planning.

Lack of state registrations. Some smaller broker-dealers may be registered in only a few states.

Dropping Your Licenses Altogether

Your final alternative involves not working through a broker-dealer at all. Under current law, you can circumvent a lot of rules and regulations when you just drop your licenses completely and become a Registered Investment Adviser. The freedom of this can be seductive to many advisers. They get to have their own name on the sign, keep 100 percent of their revenue, and manage things as they see fit. Running their business becomes much more straightforward without many of the regulatory requirements of a broker-dealer and innumerable securities laws to follow. Life becomes simple: Just provide investment advice and charge a fee.

That's the upside. However, you have to weigh it against the negatives, which are many:

- Because you'll be precluded from selling a lot of products—anything that carries a load or commission, including most insurance choices—you'll lose important flexibility in terms of being able to offer clients exactly what they need. As you've seen, this may be critical to serving the affluent market.

- If you currently have a client base from which you're receiving any type of commission income, that will stop. Unless you've designed your practice from day one to work on fees, you'll need to put a lot of effort into converting existing clients or attracting new clients. You'll find that some clients don't want to work in a fee environment at all.

- Although there is much less regulatory oversight of Registered Investment Advisers right now, you can't count on this continuing indefinitely. We believe, in fact, that the regulatory complexity will grow significantly over the next few years.
- Once you give up your license, it's hard to ever go back. The exams aren't getting any easier each year. We know many advisers who were once huge proponents of fees who dropped their licenses, who now want to be able to work with some products on a commission basis again. They're finding they can't go back because the exams are standing in the way.
- When you're selling stocks and bonds, someone else— your discount clearing platform—gets the commissions and reward for your work, not you. In addition, your client is now their client.
- When the market is rising and client portfolios are increasing in value, it's easy to justify your fees. But when the market slides, it becomes a much harder task.

The issue of fees versus commissions has been the topic of hot debates for a long time, and we don't expect the arguments to ever go away. The important question here in making your broker-dealer decision is not which is right, but which is right for you.

CHAPTER 9 # A View from the Inside: Evaluating Potential Broker-Dealers

W HEN IT COMES TO finding the right broker-dealer, we've had the benefit of seeing it from two vantage points: We've been advisers ourselves, and we've helped other advisers choose new broker-dealers through our work at our own broker-dealer. This perspective has taught us over and over the importance of making a rational, systematic assessment of your choices in order to find the best match, while at the same time listening to what your instinct tells you.

In this chapter, we cover:
- how to discover what any broker-dealer you are considering has to offer you.
- the key questions you should ask before joining a broker-dealer.

The Best Surprise Is No Surprise

THE LAST SITUATION you want to find yourself in is to have gone through the entire process of choosing and transitioning to a new broker-dealer only to find that it isn't actually a good match after all. You don't want to find out too late that it's not licensed to sell insurance in your state or that it has a corporate policy about not offering a particular investment you use.

How do you go about preventing any unexpected surprises? We believe there's no substitute for face-to-face contact. Personally visit any broker-dealer you're seriously considering, as well as, if possible, the clearing firms with which they work. Talk to advisers currently with the firm. When possible, talk to wholesalers who have done business with the broker-dealer. Every viewpoint is important.

As you have these conversations, consider that you could be operating with a set of blinders that you don't even know exists. We've found that when advisers look at new broker-dealers, they tend to evaluate them according to what was missing from the previous relationship. If they're with a wire house, they'll look for payout because that's what they're not getting at the wire house. If they're coming from a large independent broker-dealer, they may be looking for better service because they may have had a bad service experience with the big firm. Or if the advisers are currently with a firm using antiquated technology systems when they themselves are more technologically advanced, they could be looking for more sophisticated technology.

More important, we also see many advisers who are thinking about switching assume that they will get to keep everything they currently have—they take the good things for granted. We've seen advisers assume, for example, that

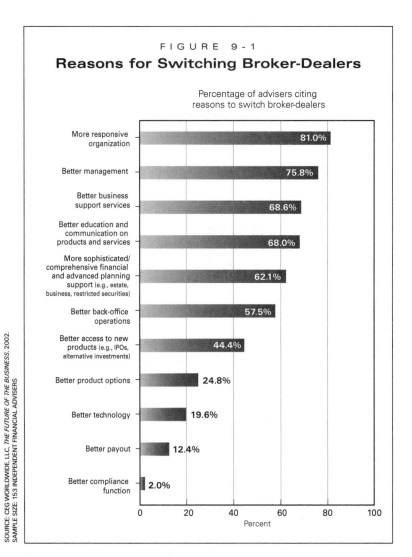

FIGURE 9-1

Reasons for Switching Broker-Dealers

Percentage of advisers citing
reasons to switch broker-dealers

Reason	Percent
More responsive organization	81.0%
Better management	75.8%
Better business support services	68.6%
Better education and communication on products and services	68.0%
More sophisticated/ comprehensive financial and advanced planning support (e.g., estate, business, restricted securities)	62.1%
Better back-office operations	57.5%
Better access to new products (e.g., IPOs, alternative investments)	44.4%
Better product options	24.8%
Better technology	19.6%
Better payout	12.4%
Better compliance function	2.0%

Percent

SOURCE: CEG WORLDWIDE, LLC. *THE FUTURE OF THE BUSINESS*, 2002.
SAMPLE SIZE: 153 INDEPENDENT FINANCIAL ADVISERS

just because they get their statements delivered electroni-
cally by their current clearing firm, that all clearing firms
will do so.

So when you look at your reasons for switching, be
aware that you're probably sensitive around certain issues.

For some perspective, it's helpful to understand why others choose to change their broker-dealer. Research from CEG Worldwide (**FIGURE 9-1**) shows the top reasons cited by independent advisers for moving.

The Make-or-Break Factors

AS YOU EVALUATE different broker-dealers, go through a laundry list of issues with each one so that you can systematically compare apples to apples. Walk through your day as an adviser and look at what you like and want to stay the same, and what you dislike and want to change. We suggest you pay very close attention to each of the following factors.

The Culture

As we've said before, relationships are everything in this business. If you're focused on building long-term relationships with your clients, you need a broker-dealer focused on building a long-term relationship with you, both as an adviser and as a person. You'll need to have a thorough understanding of the people associated with the broker-dealer to find out if they're a good match for you and your business.

Start with the management. How long have they been in business? What are their backgrounds? Have they ever worked as advisers themselves? What is the turnover of the senior managers? If there's not a lot of turnover, you can probably bet that senior management is dedicated to building the broker-dealer over the long haul.

Do they have good reputations? Are they people you can trust? Do they have a vision of where they're taking the firm and an understanding of how that vision has evolved? Do they take a personal interest in making sure issues are addressed and problems solved? These questions are important even if you're talking to a large broker-dealer where senior management is not in routine contact with advisers, because their character and attitude will trickle down throughout the organization.

If it's a smaller broker-dealer where the principals are accessible to prospective advisers, make a point to meet and spend some time with them. Are they people who are genuinely concerned with helping the advisers in their firm build their businesses? Do they listen to you carefully and answer your questions thoughtfully? Are you comfortable with them? Do you share common interests outside of work that can form the basis for a personal relationship?

Don't hesitate to ask the tough questions: If you have a particular problem, how would the broker-dealer help you? Of the advisers who have left the broker-dealer, why did they leave? There's no doubt they'll try to spin any negative situation, but you should be able to see through some of it. The responses to these kinds of questions should reveal a lot to you about how the culture operates.

It's also important that the other advisers in the broker-dealer are a good fit with you and your practice. What is the average annual gross revenue generated by advisers in the firm? It should either be similar to your own or be an amount that you plan to reach. What about their experience, client markets, and goals? If you share some common ground with these advisers, they'll be able to challenge you and help you grow. It's well worth repeating that if you don't have a community of other advisers to brainstorm with, you're going to be at a major disadvantage to those who have an active network of other advisers.

Finally, look at how the broker-dealer handles the issue of control. With so much competition among broker-dealers for the top advisers these days, they sometimes want to control their advisers' flow of information. Some try to inhibit any communication between their advisers, fearing that they will form alliances with one another and end up moving as a group to a new broker-dealer. From the advisers' perspective, however, it simply deprives them of important networking opportunities.

Sometimes a broker-dealer will restrict advisers' access to the clearing firm, worried that the advisers will come to see the clearing firm, and not the broker-dealer, as their primary partner. Ultimately, it is concerned that this would give the clearing firm more leverage in any kind of negotiation, and possibly make it very difficult for the broker-dealer to switch clearing firms.

Other broker-dealers require their advisers to run every single service item through the broker-dealer (and not through the clearing firm) because they see this service work as the primary way they add value. This can be very constricting to the elite advisers who know how and want to take care of service issues themselves directly with their clearing firms (when their clearing firms allow it). The broker-dealer in these cases may just become another hurdle they need to clear to resolve service problems.

Products

What does the product list look like? Check out everything that you use now or may possibly use in the future, including individual securities, mutual funds, annuities, managed accounts, separate accounts, hedge funds, private equity, and life insurance. You need to make sure the broker-dealer will support your work with the affluent, so find out if it has advanced tools you need for the high-net-worth market available to you.

Does the broker-dealer have in-depth knowledge about and interest in the kinds of investments, insurance, or financial strategies you offer to your clients? What is the process used for approving investments? How experienced are the people who investigate investments? Are there incentives to sell proprietary products?

Don't assume that everything you may need is available. If you have a particular approach you use often, like options strategies or work with a particular annuity, you'd better check ahead of time that the broker-dealer can handle your strategy. This is particularly important if you have a special niche business narrowly focused on one product.

The very first adviser with our broker-dealer came to us precisely because his former broker-dealer did not support his business strategy. Jill met this adviser, who primarily sold one favorite insurance product, at a weekend due diligence conference sponsored by the insurance company. When this adviser returned to his office on the following Monday, he found out that his broker-dealer had been sold over the weekend to a large insurance company and would no longer allow him to offer what had suddenly become a competing product to the parent company. He contacted Jill, found out that his product was on our product list, and became an adviser with our firm.

Also, be sure to find out if the broker-dealer will let you sell products through any side business you may have. For instance, if you sell fixed insurance products through your own insurance agency, make sure that, if you choose, you can continue to do so at your new broker-dealer. Some will allow it; if so, find out how to make appropriate disclosures to them. Many others will not, however, saying, "If you want to run your business through us, you have to run *all* your business through us."

Technology

Look at the kind of resources the broker-dealer is devoting to technology. Is it aggressively building new tools? To what extent (if any) does it involve the advisers in developing new technology—does it actively solicit input about what the advisers really need, or does it operate largely in a vacuum?

Get a complete demo of the broker-dealer's technology to see for yourself if it offers what you need. As you evaluate the system, be sure to ask the following questions:

- Is the platform easy to use, with a clear layout and quick response?
- Does it allow you to enter trade orders, or will you have to call in to the broker-dealer to have it place the trade?
- Does it provide AIMR-compliant portfolio reports so you can give your clients accurate, legally presented performance reports?
- Does it provide investment planning tools, like client profiling and asset allocation?
- Does it provide investment product analysis and comparison tools?
- Does it let clients pull up their account information and documents online?
- Does it pull together consolidated statements from all of the mutual funds you have, including those that are not with the broker-dealer's clearing firm?
- Can you use it to track your service requests, so that when you call the broker-dealer with a problem you can follow up on how it's being resolved?
- Does it include a robust contact management system that will let you cross-reference and contact clients from different systems?

- Will it let you scan clients' documents (such as wills and trusts) into your online files?
- Does it let you view your commission statements?
- Does it handle fee-based work?
- Will it interface with other software that you currently use?
- Will it allow you to go paperless?
- Can you access it remotely?
- What kind of training and ongoing support is available?

Payout

Get a complete payout schedule of all products. Find out if the payout is less if you fail to do a particular volume. Many payouts are structured to increase incrementally as your production increases. On the RIA side, is there one payout for asset management and a different payout for financial planning? If you don't ask about this specifically, you may often only be told the top payout. Also, find out how you'll be paid and how often.

It's very important to evaluate payouts in the context of what the broker-dealer has to offer. Moving to a broker-dealer paying an above-average payout won't make sense if it doesn't have exactly the support or products you need. Conversely, if you are primarily interested in a broker-dealer that will quickly and efficiently process your business, and don't need or want many support services, payout may be more important to you because you won't want to have to pay for the bells and whistles.

Service and Support

Every single broker-dealer will tell you that it excels in service, so this is perhaps the most challenging area to evaluate. The best way we've found is to ask for referrals from the broker-dealer to one or two advisers who have a mix of products and services that is similar to your own. Ask careful questions, because it's poor service, above all else, that will get you into trouble with clients. If your broker-dealer's service department can't fix something, you'll quickly find out just how little patience clients have in this area.

We were contacted by one adviser who came to us with a mark on her U-4 form (the application to register as an adviser with the NASD) caused solely by a service glitch at her former broker-dealer. A client had requested a trade, which she did, but then changed his mind and wanted out of the trade. She asked her broker-dealer's service department to undo the trade, but it didn't do it. She ended up making repeated calls over many months in an attempt to get it fixed, but the service department never took care of it. The client got so angry that he ended up filing a complaint against her.

So it's important to get things done right the first time. When a service person at your broker-dealer tells you, "I took care of it," you need to be able to believe that he really did. If you can't trust the service department and have to keep following up yourself to ensure that it was taken care of, you'll spend way too much time on non-revenue-producing work.

Look at the service model the broker-dealer employs. When you have a service request, will you have to just take a number and wait in line? This might be expected if the broker-dealer is servicing large numbers of advisers who have frequent service issues. But if you're an elite adviser, you've probably already structured your office to take care of the vast majority of service issues in-house. For those rare occasions when you do need help and attention from your broker-dealer's service department, you may be able to find a firm that can work with you and prioritize your requests.

Besides general service, look at the specific types of support the broker-dealer may offer, including:

Transitioning support. What kind of assistance does it provide to help you move? Does it have dedicated systems and staff to ease your transition? Does it make financial support available?

Marketing support. What programs does it have available to help you market more effectively? How successful have these programs been? Some large broker-dealers offer help for creating proposals, for example, or have turnkey seminar systems they will give to their advisers or sell at a discounted cost. Of course, the support you need will really depend on your business model and experience. When you need it, it's great to have. But if you don't need it, maybe you won't want to pay for it.

Practice management support. Will the broker-dealer give you help in setting up your business processes? How about coaching or assistance with staff training or time management? Again, look at what you really need, because if you choose a broker-dealer that offers support you don't need, you'll probably still pay for it.

Errors and omissions coverage. Does the broker-dealer have E and O coverage? (Some, surprisingly, do not have it.) Is the coverage adequate to cover the number of advisers it has? What are the limits and deductibles?

Costs

Ask for a complete fee schedule. Look at the standard costs, such as your ticket charges, but also look at all the little extras where you could get nickeled-and-dimed. For example, is there a monthly fee just to be with the broker-dealer? What is the E and O cost? What does the fidelity bond cost? Is there a set-up charge for the technology? Is there a monthly fee for the technology? Some firms might charge you $250 a month just to help with technology, whereas others charge nothing.

Compliance

What kind of experience and training does the compliance department staff have? Is the department fully staffed to be able to turn your requests around quickly? What is the process for getting advertising or marketing material approved? Can they help you improve your materials? Will it get turned around in twenty-four hours, or go into a black hole where you don't see it again for three weeks?

What is their attitude toward advisers? Are they flexible and willing to show you how to do something legally and safely, or do they stick to rigid company rules that are nonnegotiable? Run some scenarios by the compliance staff to gauge their flexibility and decision-making process. Do they respond automatically, or do they consider the question and all its ramifications thoughtfully?

Most important, do they use procedures that will work in the real world? Compliance people often know little about a particular product because they've never sold it and have never had to answer to clients about it. Skilled compliance departments, though, will create procedures that satisfy the dictates of the rules while meeting the needs of the adviser and client.

The Clearing Firm

You want the clearing firm to have an excellent reputation for providing solid service. Especially when you are working with affluent clients, you need to have a clearing firm where you can get things done. Because the client statements come out of the clearing firm, you want a name that is trusted by investors. It should also offer your clients high levels of account coverage to ensure that securities are returned to the clients in the event that the clearing firm would become insolvent.

Look closely at the features of the clearing firm that will affect your daily activities. How about investment research—does it offer the reports, charting, and analytical tools you want? Does it have in-house research analysts? If so, are the analysts accessible? (For example, does it have a liaison person between the analysts and advisers?) Can you use your own brand name on the clearing firm's statements, or will just your broker-dealer's name appear?

Is it known for having an excellent service team? Don't automatically assume that any service problems that you are currently experiencing lie with your broker-dealer's clearing firm. Find out if the problems are actually with the clearing firm or if they are with your current broker-dealer's service department.

Also, weigh in the fact that transitioning to a new broker-dealer that uses the same clearing firm as your current broker-dealer will be considerably easier—for both you and your clients—than moving to a broker-dealer with a new clearing firm. At the same time, just because you can get a particular product through your clearing firm now, don't assume that it will automatically be available through another broker-dealer that uses the same firm. The availability will depend on each broker-dealer's agreement with its clearing firm, as well as the broker-dealer's opinion as to which services it wants to offer.

Registered Investment Adviser

Can you have your own RIA, or do you have to use the broker-dealer's corporate RIA? If you can have your own, what are the costs and rules? How is the RIA compliance oversight cost billed by the broker-dealer? Does it charge to oversee everything from money management to financial planning, or just on certain aspects of RIA activity? Are its charges a percent of assets, a flat fee, or an hourly fee for supervision? We even know of one broker-dealer that requires advisers who want to establish their own RIA to pay a substantial fee—$25,000—which effectively discourages the advisers from doing so. Conversely, some broker-dealers are supportive of adviser-owned RIAs and have made accommodations to effectively supervise them.

Although many advisers think that broker-dealers have no liability for—and therefore no responsibility for—an RIA outside the broker-dealer, it's important to be aware that the NASD has indicated that broker-dealers do indeed have some oversight responsibility on outside RIAs, depending on the activities. This puts broker-dealers in the awkward position of having to supervise business that is not directly running through their firms in terms of oversight or payment of fees. To understand these requirements more fully, we suggest that you refer to the NASD's Notice to Members 96-33 and 94-44, as well as NASD Conduct Rule 3040. Always carefully read your firm's written supervisory procedures so you know what you can and can't do. Finally, don't assume you are covered for your RIA on your broker-dealer's E and O insurance—you may need your own separate policy, and it can be pricey.

Ongoing Contact

How will your relationship with the broker-dealer move forward once you begin to work with it? Are you required to attend meetings on a regular basis, perhaps quarterly? Some broker-dealers make such meetings mandatory, others make them optional, and some offer none at all. Is the level of contact offered by the broker-dealer appropriate for you?

What about the quality of these meetings? Are the conferences really worth your time out of the office because they provide valuable training or new sales opportunities within the broker-dealer, or are they just a waste of time? Some broker-dealers make their adviser conferences profit items, holding them in inexpensive areas and bringing in an overabundance of sponsors that pay to be there. Others provide first-rate conferences that offer important networking opportunities with top advisers.

CHAPTER 10 # Making the Change: Transitioning to a New Broker-Dealer

AS AN INDEPENDENT ADVISER, changing to a new broker-dealer is no small undertaking. We've been through it ourselves and have helped many other advisers through it, and have learned some valuable lessons from those experiences. If you follow our suggestions in this chapter, we believe you could save yourself thousands of dollars and many headaches.

To help make your transition as pain-free as possible, we show you how to:

- depart from your old broker-dealer while bringing your clients along and keeping service interruptions to a minimum.
- get settled into working with your new broker-dealer and back in business as quickly as possible.

Out with the Old

EVEN THOUGH you are looking forward to beginning to work with the new broker-dealer, you'll make the transition process much easier if you take the time to make some key preparations while you're still with your old broker-dealer.

Allow Plenty of Lead Time

We suggest you allow at least twelve weeks from the time you choose your new broker-dealer and initiate the move until your target date for switching. If you have a large office and an extensive client base, plan on even more.

If you have nonbrokerage assets only, you'll have fewer time constraints. But if you have brokerage accounts with involvement by both a clearing firm and your broker-dealer, you'll be much more subject to their time constraints. Some of the clearing firms, for example, can have huge waiting lists to facilitate transfers, some ranging from six to ten weeks, so plan to get in line in time.

In addition, your new broker-dealer may not have the proper licenses in all states, especially if it's a smaller regional firm. You'll need to allow at least several weeks (or even months) for these to be set up. Sometimes it can be longer, and if the broker-dealer has regulatory blemishes, it may never happen.

If You Need It, Get Legal Advice

You need to be very aware of the current regulators' rules and what any contract you may have with the broker-dealer says in regard to contacting and transferring clients. (This is important if you are an independent adviser; if you're an employee of a wire house, bank, or insurance company, it goes doubly so.) Dust off your copy of your contract with your broker-dealer and see what you're required to do when you leave. You may have a thirty-day written notice requirement, for instance, and an obligation to return certain books, records, and documents.

If you're an independent sole practitioner simply going from one broker-dealer to another, you'll go through a relatively routine process and may feel that you don't require assistance from an attorney. However, if there are any complicating factors, particularly if you anticipate any problems from your old broker-dealer, or if you have any partnership issues, we strongly suggest you consider hiring an attorney to negotiate the finer points of the transition. Of advisers transitioning to our own broker-dealer, half or more need the assistance of an attorney.

If you have any pending complaints or disciplinary actions, absolutely consult with an attorney—your new broker-dealer is going to be very interested in hearing all about the situation.

Prepare Complete Client Information

You need an accurate and complete record of your clients, their assets, and how to reach them, as well as contact information for all your prospects. If you're an independent adviser, check your broker-dealer contract to see if the hard-copy documentation of all this information belongs to you or to your broker-dealer. (If you're an employee, all client documentation belongs to your employer. If you try to take it with you—even copies—you could be prosecuted for theft.)

The effort that you've put into general client communication up to this point will really pay off here— the extent to which you've kept your records up-to-date and been in good contact with clients will largely determine your success in bringing them along with you to your new broker-dealer.

If you are an independent adviser working in a branch office, or a member of a partnership, plan in advance for how you'll reach an agreement with your colleagues about whose clients are whose. It's not unusual for other advisers to claim your clients as their own during a transition period.

Get the Message Out

It's common for advisers to lose some portion of their clients whenever they move to a new broker-dealer. Your goal underlying everything you do as you transition should be to keep as many clients as possible overall, and every single one of your top clients.

Two things will dictate how successful you'll be at this. The first is how well you've built client relationships over time. If you've been in frequent communication and have solidly established yourself as their trusted adviser, you're likely to keep nearly all of your clients. But if you haven't bothered to be in touch for three years, you can bet that many of your clients won't bother to follow you to your new broker-dealer.

The second thing that will determine how many clients you keep is the way you handle your communication with them throughout the transition. We suggest you start by sending out an initial explanatory letter, followed up by phone calls and additional letters.

The initial letter explaining your move should be carefully crafted. If appropriate, you may tell the clients that, although you're very happy with your relationship with your current firm, you feel that the move will provide them with new services and opportunities. Acknowledge that there is paperwork to sign and offer to talk or meet with them at any time to help walk through any issues they may have. Assure them that nothing will change in your relationship with them. Include with this letter all the paperwork the clients will need to transfer their accounts.

Keep in mind that the NASD requires you to obtain "positive consent" from clients to move brokerage accounts. This means you must receive the signed paperwork confirming that they want to remain with you. (In the past, some firms allowed you to use "negative consent," which allowed you basically to say in writing to the client, "If I don't hear from you, I'm going to assume that you're letting me move your account.") As of this writing, the "positive consent" rule applies only to brokerage accounts and not accounts held directly with mutual fund or annuity companies. Regulatory rules are a moving target, so this is another area where you might want legal advice.

Besides instructing them on how to move their accounts, your letter should let clients know if their account statements will change because of your move. If your clearing firm is not changing, let them know that their statements will probably remain nearly or exactly the same. If your new broker-dealer works with a different clearing firm, alert your clients they will have to go through the account transfer process (known as "ACAT"), and that their new statements and envelopes will look different. Often the clearing firms have pamphlets available to help clients familiarize themselves with the new statements, which you can include with your letter. You might also consider offering a class on reading the new statements to clients who want it—this is a good chance to introduce your service staff to your clients.

Finally, your letter should let clients know that they will probably receive two sets of end-of-the-year tax documents, for the dividends, interest, and capital gains they received when they were with each firm.

The timing on sending the letter is important, and you should be ready to act as quickly as possible in transferring accounts, starting from the moment you leave a broker-dealer. Consider timing your move so that your last day at the firm is a Friday, giving notice in writing to the proper supervisor. This gives you the weekend to get the initial letter and paperwork out to clients. (Even better, a three-day weekend may help you reach more clients before the markets reopen.)

You may want to overnight your letters to your top clients so that they receive them on Saturday, and then follow up immediately with phone calls and, if appropriate, visits to their homes to collect the signed documents. If you move aggressively, there may be a period of only a few days when your top accounts are not under your name.

For all other clients, follow up your letter with a phone call in the week following your move. Confirm that they received the letter and answer any questions they may have. Encourage them to return the paperwork to you as soon as possible in order for you to continue to monitor and service their accounts. In the following weeks, send out additional letters to those clients who have not yet transferred. You may want to let them know that you're doing well and settled in at the new firm, and remind them again about signing and returning the documents.

It's worth repeating here that these guidelines are for independent advisers—employees of wire houses, banks, and insurance companies generally cannot contact their old clients, per their registered representative or employment agreements.

Bridge the Gap Between Old and New

Realize that a gap—from a day or so up to a couple of weeks—when you are no longer the adviser on some or all client accounts is going to be nearly unavoidable. Structure your transition to narrow the gap as much as you can and, if possible, to still be able to take care of clients during this period.

A very effective way to close the gap is to announce your move to clients before you actually terminate your license. This gives your clients time to return their paperwork to you immediately after the date you actually switch, and allows you to begin to transfer accounts starting from your first day of business with the new broker-dealer.

Your ability to do an early announcement will depend on a couple of things. First, you'll have to have a great relationship with your broker-dealer, otherwise it will be unwilling to let you tell your clients that you're moving to another broker-dealer while you're still with it. Second, the broker-dealer will need to have a compliance stance that is flexible enough to allow it. Many have rigid rules around transitioning that would prevent this type of open communication with your clients.

You may also be able to leave one licensed staff person behind at your old broker-dealer for thirty or sixty days to service client accounts after you've moved. Your ability to do this will again depend on how friendly your relationship is with the broker-dealer.

If you are not changing clearing firms and the bulk of your accounts are held there, you should try to negotiate use of the technology to view the old brokerage accounts for at least ninety days after your move. No matter how far in advance you've planned your transition, there will still always be dividends, interest, and capital gains hitting the old accounts for some time, and you'll want to be able to check on these and ensure that they get transferred. Keep in mind that viewing old accounts may not be possible due to many factors, including technology issues (if you're changing clearing firms) or privacy concerns on the part of the old broker-dealer for those clients.

Finally, minimize client inconvenience by not initiating transfers or exchanges right before you move. You don't want clients to be in the middle of a transfer when you're changing broker-dealers. Also, avoid a tax season transition—nothing would be worse than clients bouncing checks from their brokerage checking accounts to the IRS just because you are changing broker-dealers. Likewise, moving in December can be inconvenient because clients' accounts may be frozen for a few days right at the time they might like to do end-of-the-year trades for tax purposes.

Be a Class Act

The most professional advisers we know are up-front with their broker-dealer about why they are leaving, and strive to maintain a good relationship throughout their transition and beyond. The best broker-dealers will handle your exit professionally in return. After all, they want to leave the door open in case you ever decide to come back, and they probably don't want you saying bad things about them once you leave.

It's best to frame the move as being best for everyone. For example, the clients will be better served in a different environment, or you are growing in ways that are better served at a new firm. If you've had a good relationship with the folks at the broker-dealer, there's much less chance that there will be any animosity. When they know you well, they will understand that the change is right for you.

By all means, don't burn your bridges. We once had an adviser who was transitioning to our broker-dealer show us the letter she was planning to send her clients. In it, she spent a full three pages complaining about her existent broker-dealer. We explained that, because she was still technically licensed with that broker-dealer, they would have to approve the letter. Politically, this would have been suicide for her at a time when she still needed the current broker-dealer's help.

Send out a letter on your last day with your soon-to-be former broker-dealer, letting the key people at that broker-dealer know that you enjoyed working with them and wishing them success in the future. Keep to the high road, because you'll inevitably see these people again. They could end up working at your new broker-dealer, or even acquiring your new broker-dealer. With the rapid change in the industry, you never know whom you'll be working with in the future.

In with the New

YOUR FIRST STEP in working with your new broker-dealer should be to look ahead all the way to a possible departure and negotiate exit terms. Like a prenuptial agreement, you want to ensure that your best interests are preserved no matter how the relationship unfolds. Regardless of how good you may feel about the people at the new broker-dealer, you can't assume that your situation won't change—there could easily be a shift in the ownership or management after you join the broker-dealer.

Determine whether the broker-dealer will help you transfer your clients if you leave, such as by facilitating block transfers of your nonbrokerage accounts. Negotiate the ability to take copies of all the appropriate client documents with you. Everything about what your departure would look like should be spelled out and included in your registered representative agreement.

Once this has been handled, you'll be ready to move ahead with the nuts and bolts of doing business with the broker-dealer. The broker-dealer should have a game plan laid out for you, letting you know everything that is required and who is responsible for what, and give you regular updates on the status of each step.

You can make the process flow more smoothly and quickly on your end by dedicating one of your staff members to facilitate the transfer. Don't kid yourself here. As an adviser, you excel at relationship management and solution development, not the detailed, nitty-gritty service work your transition will require. Get your service team involved—you need to be working with clients to keep the cash flowing throughout the process.

The following are the major tasks you'll need to take care of in order to complete the transition:

Consolidate your business information. Your new broker-dealer will need you to gather and submit a range of data about your business, including its legal name, names of all staff people, and the licenses they hold.

Create new marketing materials. This includes your letterhead and business cards, as well as any new brochures or advertising you need right away. These must all be submitted for approval to the new broker-dealer's compliance department. You'll also need to account for production and printing time.

Assemble a master list of all mutual fund and insurance products currently used by clients. You and the broker-dealer will need this list to ensure that the broker-dealer has selling agreements and proper licensing in place for all of your clients' different accounts. This list should be easy if you've kept up with the technology.

Get ready to transfer your licenses. Your new broker-dealer will take care of this process, including completing and transmitting your Central Registration Depository (CRD) forms to the NASD. You will need to pay new NASD and state licensing fees (which are not prorated for the year), however, as well as be fingerprinted again. If your NASD registration form (Form U-4) is clean, the licenses can be transferred in a day. But if you have regulatory or client complaint disclosures on it, it could take days, weeks, or even months due to regulatory review.

Review the Written Supervisory Procedures. The WSP inevitably will be different at your new broker-dealer. Read and understand it, because the last thing you want to do to your clients after moving them to a new firm is to make embarrassing procedural service mistakes or a compliance misstep.

Set up new technology. Work with the broker-dealer to get your new systems installed and running and arrange for you and your staff to be trained to use them.

CHAPTER 11 **Look Before You Leave: Going Independent**

MOVING FROM being an employee to being self-employed in your own business represents a tremendous amount of effort and risk, but the rewards can be well worth it. We've seen many, many advisers in recent years strike out from their employers to build flourishing practices in the independent sector.

But going independent isn't for everyone. To make the best decision, you need to do a full self-assessment in light of the challenges you'll face, and be fully aware of the tasks you'll have to undertake in order to set up your new business.

It boils down to two important questions, which we help you answer in this chapter:

- Am I right for going independent?
- If so, how do I prepare to go into business for myself?

Are You Ready to Be
an Independent Adviser?

YOUR DECISION ABOUT going independent is a matter of taking a rational look at the advantages an independent business would give you and then weighing those against the drawbacks of leaving your wire house, bank, or insurance company.

First, you'll enjoy a high level of autonomy. You'll make your own decisions about the course of your business, and whether or not you succeed will be entirely up to you. You'll no longer be required to represent proprietary products and so will have the flexibility to structure portfolios precisely the way you want to match clients' needs. You'll have no sales quotas (although you may need to meet revenue minimums) and no pressure to add clients.

You'll have the freedom to market yourself as you wish, positioning yourself to attract the clients you want to work with. You won't be faced with wire house, bank, or insurance company rules that prohibit you from prospecting someone who is already a client with another adviser in the firm.

With higher payouts, you'll keep much more of the revenue you generate. You'll be able to build equity in your business, turning your years of hard work building a client base into real dollars. If you choose, you can build the business to pass on to others in your family, or you can sell it in order to cash out all your equity. You'll have a business you can sell, not just a job you can retire from.

But when you go independent, you'll also lose some important benefits, many of which you may have taken for granted. You'll have no more guarantees—there's no assurance that your business will succeed, regardless of how much effort you put into it. You'll lose the prestige of your employer's name and walk away from the security of a large company. This security may include a salary, a draw, health insurance benefits, paid vacation, and a retirement plan. In many cases you'll lose the relationships you've enjoyed and will no longer have a built-in team of peers, or more important, service assistants, to work with.

You will have no more proprietary products to lean on and may have to find a new product list you feel comfortable recommending. If any clients move with you, you'll probably have to have them get rid of the proprietary products that you previously sold them, which can be uncomfortable for you and costly to the clients.

You'll face significant costs—in time and money—in setting up and running your office. You will have to begin to actively market yourself and your new company. As you're doing all this, you'll risk having legal action taken against you by your former employer.

Although you'll be out from under the structure of your employer, with this freedom comes danger. Sometimes a lack of structure makes people crumble—without being told what options to recommend to clients and which technology to use, the sheer number of choices can lead to inaction.

Does going independent still look attractive? If it looks to you like the pros outweigh the cons, you'll next need to ask: What are my chances of succeeding as an independent? We suggest you break it down into the following questions:

Do you really, really want to leave your current employer? Going independent is a little different for everyone, but we can tell you one thing for sure: It will be more work than you think. This means you need to be deeply committed and passionate about making the change. Consider the question in the context of what will truly be best for your career over the long term. You have to have more reason to move than just to escape a conflict with your current boss or to be free of some annoying corporate policy.

Have you been successful with your employer's firm? We've seen that successful wire house, bank, and insurance company advisers tend to be successful as independents, but unsuccessful ones tend to still be unsuccessful in the independent sector. If you haven't enjoyed success with your employer, don't expect that the independent environment alone will make you successful.

Do you have an entrepreneurial mind-set? Are you a risk taker? Just as important, do you have the knowledge and experience to back up your risks?

Will it be good for your clients? As an independent, will you be able to provide them with better service and more of the solutions they need? If going independent means asking your clients to accept less than what they have now, it's not the right move for you.

Do you have clients who will move with you? If you've put serious effort into building client relationships over time, these clients will be poised to move with you. If you're not close to your clients, however, they may be content to just let themselves be assigned to another broker.

Will you mind all the details of running your own office? Operating a small business will require you to wear many hats, from boss to errand runner. The idea of being in charge probably appeals to you, but how will you feel about fixing the paper jam in the copier, or paying someone else to do it for you?

Do you have enough cash? You'll need plenty of reserve to see yourself through your first six months or so of business.

Is your family on board? Do they support your decision? This is important because your move to running your own business can mean changes for them, too.

Preparing to Go Independent

THERE ARE NO two ways about it: Leaving your employer will not be easy or simple. You face a myriad of tasks big and small to launch your new business, as well as obstacles placed by your employer to prevent you from leaving.

Your goal will be to make your jump to independence as painless as it can be by careful planning, full preparation, and quick execution. Allow at least nine or ten months from the time you decide to go independent until your target date for leaving your employer to accomplish everything.

Anticipate the Blowback

Prepare to protect yourself from the ramifications of leaving. Look at the clues around you that will help you anticipate what might happen when you turn in your resignation. Have you seen anyone similar to yourself leave the organization? If so, what happened? Is there pattern or precedent that you could expect will be followed with your leaving?

What is your relationship with your branch manager? Some advisers have great relationships and the branch managers keep their hands largely off their accounts when they leave. In other cases, the branch manager may make it difficult for you in order to set an example to discourage other advisers from leaving. Likewise, the branch managers may have their own manager coming down on them to try to stop the move, and you'll face stumbling blocks at every turn.

Keep in mind that your employers will view your leaving mainly in terms of customer accounts. They won't be nearly so concerned with your departure as they will be with what may happen to their accounts as a result of you leaving.

Get Legal Help

Consult with a knowledgeable securities attorney well in advance of your planned move. (To find a good attorney, ask for referrals from your new broker-dealer or other advisers you know who have gone independent.) You'll want to first look at your contract, which will spell out the terms of your leaving and how you can contact your old clients, if at all.

Work very carefully with your attorney to figure out how to protect yourself from accusations of theft. For example, have an inventory of what you have and what you've returned. Prepare a list of all documents, books, and systems that you have returned to the firm, and get someone at the firm to sign off that they have received them. You won't be able to go back later and find any missing items for them.

Be prepared to do some legal maneuvering. Be ready to deal with a lawsuit brought against you for breach of contract, or a temporary restraining order preventing you from making any move toward contacting existing clients. In some cases, expect that you may have to pay a settlement.

Create a Business Plan

Get help from an accountant to create a pro forma income statement, plan your bookkeeping systems, and guide you with tax strategies. Even if your eyes are wide open, there will still be expenses that you can't know about in advance. As soon as you become an independent businessperson, expenses that were insignificant to you before will suddenly start to add up. Technology and marketing, for example, are two major areas where expenses can run higher than you would expect. Working with an accountant to create a plan will help you adopt the mind-set you'll need to run your new business successfully. When forecasting your revenue, be extremely realistic and err on the low side. Your payouts may be higher, but it could be quite some time from the date you open your new business until you actually receive your first check, especially if you rely on quarterly management fees. In addition, count on your production to immediately drop from where it was when you were with your previous employer, and to take longer than you think to get back to that level.

As you project your expenses, remember that it's important to put your best foot forward from the beginning. This means that you shouldn't try to run your new business on a shoestring, especially if you're working with affluent clients. Determine each of the expenses you'll incur in launching the business and then in running it from month to month. Add in a margin of error to the high side on each one.

At a minimum, include these start-up costs:

- office rent (two months' rent plus deposit)
- office equipment, including computers, printers, fax machine, copier, and telephones
- office furniture
- legal and account fees related to the start-up
- license transfer fees
- design of identity
- stationery printing

Also, factor in these ongoing costs:

- employee salaries and benefits
- office rent
- insurance

- utilities, including Internet access, phone, and electricity
- advertising, including website creation and maintenance
- annual licensing fees
- office supplies
- postage
- travel
- accounting and bookkeeping fees
- subscriptions

Set Up Your Office Wisely

You'll need to move as quickly as possible to generate revenue from the day you leave your employer, so have all the parts of your new business well in place before you go. These will be your major tasks:

- Decide where to locate your office, negotiate your lease, and get the office furnished.
- Choose, buy, and install technology, including computers, software, and peripherals.
- Create a brand identity, along with all marketing materials such as advertisements, brochures, and a website.
- If appropriate, staff your office; decide on the number and type of staff people, write job descriptions, advertise for or recruit candidates, and conduct interviews.

To save yourself some steps and do it right the first time, think about enlisting a business and marketing consultant specializing in helping financial advisers establish their practices. Your independent broker-dealer may offer these services, or be able to refer you to some good resources. Look to see what's working at the offices of other advisers from your new broker-dealer. You'll find that people with good, well-run offices are proud of them and will want to talk to you about them.

Also consider hiring an office coordinator to take care of some of the time-intensive legwork, like buying furniture, getting your letterhead printed, and overseeing the installation of your phones and computers. Because you have to have the ultimate in discretion while setting up your office—if your employer gets any inkling that you're planning on leaving, you'll probably be fired in a second—an office coordinator can be a big help.

If the idea of setting up your own office from scratch is too daunting, there are a couple of alternatives that might work for you. First, consider an office-sharing arrangement where the infrastructure is already in place. These typically involve a floor or suite of private offices that share a receptionist, secretary, and conference room and already have phone and computer systems in place. This may be more expensive than setting up your own office, but it's easy and you'll avoid having to commit to a lease on your own space. You can add adjoining offices as you grow, and the leases are usually month-to-month.

Second, you might consider joining an already established independent branch office. It can be quite comforting if you've just left an employer to be able to walk into a place where there's already a receptionist, signage, letterhead, and systems. Advisers at these firms are usually independent contractors, so this alternative can easily become a bridge to starting your own branch office if you desire. If you choose this route, we suggest you look most closely at the reputation of any firm you consider, especially how it treats clients, employees, and associates. You may want to ask attorneys, wholesalers, and accountants that work with the firm about the reputations of its principals.

Avoid the temptation to just set up the office in your home. In most instances, we've found that advisers are more successful when they work from a professional office environment. (There have been some exceptions, especially when the advisers have separate buildings on their property that they use for an office.) When we've convinced advisers to move out from their home offices, their business has increased dramatically.

Leverage Your New Broker-Dealer

Your first and best resource for setting up your new business should be your new broker-dealer.

We've seen many advisers spend the first few months after leaving their wire houses being completely overwhelmed— shell-shocked, even—by everything they have to do and learn.

Your broker-dealer can really provide some value by helping to minimize your information overload and set you on the right path. It should be able to provide help in a range of areas, including:

- recommendations for computer systems and programs.
- training of new staff people.
- assistance with business planning, including templates of costs you will encounter.
- contacts with other advisers who have made the move to independence.

To get the best help, we encourage you to share information about the plans for your new practice with your broker-dealer. We have found that advisers who are eager to tell others and gather feedback about their business plans are universally more successful than those who closely guard that information.

CHAPTER 12 **A Win-Win Situation: Building a Great Relationship with Your Broker-Dealer**

OVER THE YEARS, we've seen how hundreds of different advisers work with their broker-dealers. Some barely take advantage of the relationship, whereas others leverage it to the max. The most successful advisers consistently take the following actions to get the most out of the resources offered by their broker-dealers.

Get to Know the Key People—Face to Face

The key person could be the primary service person, it could be the regional manager, or it could even be the broker-dealer's principals. Regardless, if you personally know whom you're dealing with, it will make a huge difference in getting your problems solved. It's always much harder for people to say "no" to someone they've met.

If you're working with a smaller broker-dealer, it's also worth your while to introduce yourself to some of the back-office people. Very often the people in the back office will know your name, but otherwise never have a chance to meet you. At our own broker-dealer, we always encourage our advisers to stop by when they're in the neighborhood just to be able to meet our staff.

Ask Frequently About New Technology and Products

Be proactive about finding out about new technology your broker-dealer or its clearing firm is building, or products that are coming online. Don't miss out on a capability that they've developed (or had all along) just because you never asked and they never told you. Your broker-dealer or clearing firm may not be all that great at self-promotion and could be so busy building the new system that they neglect to tell you once it's finished.

Build Bridges to the Clearing Firm

If both your broker-dealer and the clearing firm will allow it, visit the clearing firm yourself in order to make some personal contacts. (As long as your broker-dealer is amenable to the idea, it can help you set up the visit.) You can find out a great deal from your clearing firm about its offerings and its technology that the broker-dealer may not tell you. Ask for a preview of what's being developed—you may end up saving yourself from making an investment in some new technology if you find out that the clearing firm will be offering a system that will do the same thing. In addition, as long as it makes sense for your business, try to attend conferences and training programs offered by your clearing firm.

Get Involved with the Other Advisers

As we mentioned, some firms just don't want their advisers to get to know each other. If your own broker-dealer is not

among this group, take advantage of every opportunity to
network with the other advisers and be a part of the community. Volunteer to do a welcome wagon–type follow-up
with new advisers coming on board. Offer to meet with
adviser prospects to give your perspective on the broker-
dealer. Volunteer to write articles for the broker-dealer
adviser newsletter, profiling something that's working
really well for you.

Go Easy on the Service People

The back-office people generally work long days without great pay, and being caustic to them will do little to
help you get problems solved. A little civility goes a long,
long way—you'll make these folks happy to pick up the
phone and return your calls. Compliment them when
it's deserved—a good word about them to their manager
could someday result in them going the extra mile for
you. Likewise, if you or your service staff is experiencing a
problem, let a manager know. There is often a simple communication or processing issue that can be resolved easily
between the parties.

Provide Feedback

Your broker-dealer can be a much better partner to you
if it doesn't have to guess at what you need. Let your
broker-dealer know if you're happy—or unhappy—and
why. If your broker-dealer has an adviser sounding board
committee set up to gather input, volunteer to serve on
it. Likewise, if it offers a sounding board area on its website, use it—the good broker-dealers will respond to your
input. When your broker-dealer is putting the finishing
touches on a new technology that looks like it will help
your business, volunteer to help test it. You'll come to

know it inside and out and will have a voice in helping craft the completed product.

Share Your Goals with the Appropriate Person

When we do the budget for our broker-dealer each year, we contact every office and interview each adviser about her goals for the coming year. Instead of just guessing what each office will be doing by applying some general growth rate assumptions, we specifically ask, "What do you think next year is going to bring for you?" Besides helping us tailor our operations to meet projected needs, this is an opportunity for us to find out what we can do immediately to help the advisers get started on reaching their goals.

If your own broker-dealer doesn't prompt you for this information, go out of your way to share it anyway. For example, let it know what your goals for revenue growth are for next year, where you'd like to take your technology, and how you want your office to develop. If you don't communicate what you are trying to achieve with your broker-dealer, it is probably not going to be as good a partner as it could be.

Be a True Partner

Put yourself in your broker-dealer's shoes and make an effort to understand the dynamics behind its decisions. There are some things that the firm just can't do, either from a business or a compliance standpoint. Don't expect your broker-dealer to do something for you that will make it lose money or otherwise harm the firm. Not only is that bad for the broker-dealer, in the long run it won't help you, either.

For us, the advisers who stand out are the ones who acknowledge that we're in the business for the long term and to make money (just as they are). They recognize that they won't do well unless the broker-dealer does well, too. We see these advisers as legitimate businesspeople, not just people trying to squeeze every possible benefit for themselves regardless of what it costs the broker-dealer. By approaching the relationship with a win-win attitude— that what's good for advisers has to be good for the broker-dealer, and vice versa—they become true partners, not just customers.

PART 4

The Future Awaits
Transform Your Practice

With our industry undergoing dramatic changes, the reality is that most advisers will have to transform their firms from what *used* to work to what *will* work in order to succeed. Advisers who choose to continue doing the same thing they've done year after year can no longer expect the same results. With increased competition, higher client expectations, and downward pressure on fees, they're likely to find their businesses eroding.

The challenge then is not deciding *if* you should change, but *how*. In this final section, we'll look at how to bring about the changes within your firm that will set it on course to becoming an elite financial services practice.

CHAPTER 13 **Pulling It All Together: Design for Success**

I
N THE PREVIOUS CHAPTERS, you've learned the essential strategies for building an elite practice: focusing on a select group of affluent clients, using a consultative process, building lasting client relationships, running your firm efficiently, investing in education for yourself and clients, and tapping the resources of strategic partners. You've also learned how to choose the right broker-dealer for your practice and get the most from that relationship.

You now have to translate that knowledge into action, transforming your firm into the business of your dreams. In this final chapter, we look at the two essentials for incorporating successful change into your practice:

- the value of creating a road map
- the steps to successful change

The Power of a Plan

THERE'S LITTLE DOUBT that every financial adviser is in business to succeed, to enjoy a good income, and to serve clients well. But some advisers are extremely successful, whereas so many others are just hanging on. What's the difference between these very successful and not-so-successful advisers?

More often than not, we've found that the most successful advisers are focused on what they want to achieve and how they are going to achieve it. These advisers envision their success, draw up clear plans for getting there, and then find effective ways to incorporate change into their firms.

This is borne out in research by CEG Worldwide, which finds that the average net income of advisers increases significantly as they develop a business or marketing plan. For instance, only 7.3 percent of advisers with an average net income of less than $75,000 had a business or marketing plan. In contrast, 31.4 percent of advisers taking home more than $150,000 a year had a business or marketing plan. (See FIGURE 13-1.)

We've found that these advisers intentionally position themselves to achieve success. They are successful because they:

- have a vision of what their life will be like once they achieve their goals.
- clearly define the goals that they're committed to achieving.
- continue to refine their skills through consistent practice and repetition.
- review their goals over and over again to stay focused on what is important in their lives.
- hold themselves accountable for reaching their next level of success.

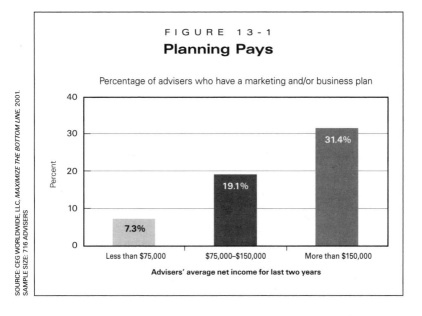

FIGURE 13-1
Planning Pays

Percentage of advisers who have a marketing and/or business plan

Don't put yourself at a disadvantage by failing to develop a plan. Without one, it's easy to become overwhelmed by the challenges you face. But by developing a business plan with goals that you are passionate about achieving, you'll remain focused on your priorities and on track to achieving your vision. Once you have an intention to succeed, many of your perceived obstacles will disappear.

Steps to Successful Change

To ACHIEVE what's important to you, you must clearly understand where you want to go and what you need to do to purposefully design your own future. The following steps will help you draw your road map and then set you on your way to successful change.

Assess Where You Are Now

Start by taking a hard look at the nuts and bolts of your business. Ask yourself the questions that will truly pinpoint the level of success that you've achieved to date. Your questions will vary according to the structure and priorities of your firm, but these would be typical:

- What are your current assets under management? Has that amount increased or decreased over the past year?
- What was your net income over the last twelve months? Is that up or down from the previous year?
- How many clients do you have? How many are affluent clients from your target market?
- Has your number of clients increased or decreased over the last twelve months?
- How many referrals have you received over the last year for prospects in your target market?
- Have you maintained consistent communication with your clients?
- Do you have systems in place that keep your business running smoothly?
- Is your technology up to date?
- Do you take full advantage of your educational and networking opportunities?
- Do you have any mutually advantageous strategic alliances in place?
- Are you satisfied with your broker-dealer relationship?

Determine Where You Want to Go

Once you've made a realistic assessment of where you are, consider exactly where you want to go. You need to be able to clearly define what you're trying to accomplish in order to keep your goals from getting lost in your daily activities and immediate concerns.

Contrast your current situation with where you would like to be within a specific, realistic time frame, such as three years from now. Is what you are doing today what really matters to you in the long run? Identify the income you would like to earn, the number and types of clients you would like to have, the amount of assets under management you would like, and any other benchmarks for the level of success you want to achieve.

It will be helpful to revisit the questions from your self-assessment. This time, identify what you want to achieve in each area in your specified time frame. For example, you may currently have no strategic alliances in place. Your goal might be to form five alliances within the next three years.

Identify the Actions You Must Take

For each goal you've defined, put together a step-by-step action plan that breaks it down into manageable tasks. For each task, describe what must be done, who is responsible for doing it, and the date that it will be completed. Make each job clearly defined and actionable.

By reducing the steps you need to take into manageable pieces, you'll help bridge the gap between the day-to-day demands of running a business and your vision of where you want to take your firm.

For instance, let's say that in three years you want to have doubled your assets under management, moved half of your clients to a fee basis, and have systems in place that will provide a high level of streamlined client service. These goals might become overwhelming if you consider all the major hurdles that must be cleared in order to reach them. However, by breaking down all the major tasks into monthly steps, they will much more easily become a reality.

Create the Commitment to Change

With your goals clearly defined, your next—and more challenging—step is to set the changes into action within your firm that will achieve your goals. If you have partners or employees, your first task will be to win a commitment to change from each of them.

Successful change is a real challenge because no one reacts well to change except the person who is driving it. When faced with change, most people tend to immediately try to figure out how to avoid it. This includes the people within your own firm.

Don't underestimate the time you will need to gain this commitment. Everyone needs time to digest and understand how the changes will affect their jobs and themselves personally. They will ask, "How is it going to affect the company?" and "How will it affect me?" Some on your team may have difficulty understanding the significance of the changes you are attempting to incorporate into the business.

In response, you need to be ready to paint a picture of what the firm is going to look like when the transformation is complete. If they can clearly see the answers to their questions, they'll be much better able and willing to help you create change. Give them both time and information so they can conclude for themselves that it is not only in the firm's best interest, but also in their own enlightened self-interest, to help make your proposed changes a reality.

You need to be able to describe how, by making specific changes, you will be able to grow significantly faster while providing your clients with better service, and how this will translate into more opportunities or rewards for them. You need to also be able to describe the ramifications of not changing, including falling behind competitors, fewer opportunities for employees, and decreased ability to provide meaningful help to your clients. With this kind of information, change should not be a very difficult decision for your staff.

Set the Change in Motion

With a clear commitment from your partners, staff, and any other stakeholders, your next step will be to begin to implement your plan. Everything you do should be consistent with the commitment, so with every action you take (or ask others to take), ask yourself if it is consistent with what you want to achieve. In so doing, you will create a new culture in your firm that welcomes and adapts to change.

Create a sense of urgency around the change. Remember —and remind others—that it's fine to be uncomfortable with change, but that the winner in business will always be the one who most effectively adjusts to the new environment.

Look Ahead

Last of all, always keep in mind that there is no "final destination." The world is always changing, and our industry along with it. Constantly reinvent yourself and your firm, seeking out new ways to tap into the ever-evolving opportunities. By anticipating and readily adapting to change, you'll set yourself apart from your competitors, provide the best possible service to your clients, and succeed in building the elite practice you deserve.

RESOURCES

NOTHING GREAT is ever built by one person alone. As we're fond of saying, relationships are everything in our business, and the following people, organizations, and publications have consistently been of tremendous help to us in building our businesses. We encourage you to explore what they have to offer you.

ASSOCIATIONS

American Institute of Certified Public Accountants (AICPA)
This association of more than 345,000 CPAs offers its members continuing education, conferences, publications, and a range of other resources, including retirement and insurance programs. For full information, visit www.aicpa.org.

The Association for Investment Management and Research (AIMR)
An international, nonprofit organization with more than 50,000 members in more than 100 countries. It offers services in three broad categories, including education, professional conduct and ethics, and standards of practice and advocacy. It also awards the Chartered Financial Analyst (CFA) accreditation to qualified advisers. For information, see www.aimr.com.

Financial Planning Association (FPA)
With its goal to foster the value of financial planning and advance the financial planning profession, the FPA's mem-

bers include financial planners as well as other professional advisers who are involved with financial planning. It offers networking opportunities, career development, and continuing education. For details, see www.fpanet.org.

Investment Management Consultants Association (IMCA)

The IMCA is devoted to providing education to investment management consultants, and to developing industry standards. It offers educational opportunities, conferences, publications, networking, and a professional certification program to its members. See www.imca.org for additional details.

Million Dollar Round Table (MDRT)

An international association of nearly 30,000 of the world's top life insurance and financial services professionals from seventy-four nations, membership in the MDRT is recognized as a standard of excellence. It provides numerous ongoing educational and networking opportunities. For more information, go to www.mdrt.org.

National Association of Insurance and Financial Advisors (NAIFA)

The NAIFA represents the interests of more than 70,000 insurance and financial advisers across the United States by encouraging legislation and regulation to ensure a healthy marketplace. It also offers its members education, training, and networking opportunities. See www.naifa.org for more information.

National Association of Personal Financial Advisors (NAPFA)

The largest association of fee-only financial advisers in the United States, NAPFA focuses on enhancing the skills of its members and educating the public about the financial planning process. Benefits include participation in its referral service, continuing education, and reduced registration fees for conferences. For details, see www.napfa.org.

Society of Financial Service Professionals

This association of 25,000 credentialed financial services professionals is dedicated to advancing the professionalism of members to enable them to better serve their clients. The Society requires members to have earned one or more of eleven qualifying professional credentials and offers education, networking, and professional resources. Visit www.financialpro.org for more information.

COACHES

Bill Bachrach

Author of *Values-Based Selling* (Bachrach & Associates Inc., 1996) and *High-Trust Leadership* (Aim High Publishing, 1999), Bill is an influential industry thinker. He offers many tools for advisers, including a monthly newsletter, seminars, a coaching program, and a study group. His website at www.bachrachvbs.com has additional details.

John Bowen

John is a leading expert on the financial services industry, helping both advisers and the institutions that serve them to become more profitable. He also is the author of *Creating Equity: How to Build a Hugely Profitable Asset Management Business* (Securities Data Publishing Books, 1997). His research and consulting firm, CEG Worldwide, makes a number of valuable resources available to advisers, including white papers on best adviser practices; e-mail newsletters; one-day seminars; and a year-long, in-depth coaching program. Complete information can be found on the CEG Worldwide website at www.cegworldwide.com.

Tom Gau

Tom helps advisers in a number of areas, including practice management, marketing, and client service. Active on the speaking circuit, he also conducts seminars and offers other training material through his company, Million Dollar Producer. More information is available at www.mdproducer.com.

Steve Moeller

We believe that Steve's book, *Effort-Less Marketing for Financial Advisors* (American Business Visions, 1999), is a great marketing guidebook. His firm, American Business Visions, makes several resources available to advisers, including a free newsletter, a coaching program, and turnkey marketing systems. See www.businessvisions.com for additional details.

Dan Sullivan

Creator of the *Strategic Coach* program, Dan is of great help to advisers and other entrepreneurs seeking better focus and balance in their businesses and lives. In addition to his coaching programs, he offers books, audiotapes, and software. Full details are at www.strategiccoach.com.

SPEAKER/CONSULTANTS

Bill Acheson

Bill is an outstanding public speaking consultant whom we've found valuable and who is available by arrangement to individual advisers. He can be reached at 724-538-4910.

Harry S. Dent

An investment strategist and author of several books, including the bestseller *The Roaring 2000s* (Simon & Schuster, 1998), Harry is a great source of tools and ideas for helping clients understand economic change and its impact. He publishes a monthly newsletter, the *H.S. Dent Forecast,* as well as a range of excellent client education materials including audiotapes and research reports. For more information, see www.hsdent.com.

Bill Good

An old friend, Bill has been of incredible assistance to us in the areas of marketing and productivity. Through his company, Bill Good Marketing, he offers a number of different tools, including prospecting and client communication systems, seminars, and tapes. He speaks widely at industry events and is also the author of *Prospecting Your Way to Sales Success* (Scribner, 1997). For more information, see www.billgood.com.

Kip Gregory

Kip coaches individuals and sales teams on how to leverage desktop and Internet technology to increase their productivity and strengthen their relationships. His free e-mail newsletter, *Kip's Tips,* is devoted to the best websites and software for financial advisers. For details, visit www.gregory-group.com.

Nick Murray

Nick is a great source of ideas and inspiration for financial advisers, whom we've known for many years. He is the author of several books for financial advisers, including *The New Financial Advisor* (The Nick Murray Company, Inc.,

2001); offers intensive, one-day master classes for advisers; and directs a newsletter/spot coaching service for advisers entitled *Nick Murray Interactive*. More information can be found at www.nickmurray.com.

Leo Pusateri

Leo and his team at Pusateri Consulting & Training offer strategic consulting to both individuals and organizations in the financial services industry. They specialize in helping clients to discover and articulate their unique value in order to set themselves apart from their competition. Find more information at www.pusatericonsulting.com.

Chip Roame

Chip is one of the top strategy consultants in our industry. Although he usually works with financial institutions, he will on occasion work with top financial advisers. His website at www.tiburonadvisors.com has additional details.

Mark Tibergien

Mark, who works with accounting firm Moss Adams, is considered one of the leading experts on business valuation and succession. A summary of services is available at www.mossadams.com/services/bizconsulting/succession.

TOOLS

Kolbe Corp.

Kolbe has produced a number of different tests designed to match individuals, their talents, and their instincts with the right kind of work. We use the Kolbe A Index test to help us identify people with the natural capabilities to enjoy certain work. Contact them at www.kolbe.com.

National Association of Professional Organizers (NAPO)
For organizationally challenged advisers, this association of organization experts can be of great value. Through its website at www.napo.net, you can request a referral to a local member who can help you get organized so that your focus is on revenue-producing activities.

Toastmasters
This organization can be extremely helpful to advisers looking to improve their public speaking skills. To locate a Toastmasters chapter in your area, visit www.toast masters.org.

MAGAZINES, NEWSPAPERS, AND NEWSLETTERS

Advisor Today
The official publication of the National Association of Insurance and Financial Advisors, this monthly magazine covers a wide range of topics, including life and health insurance, financial advising, and practice management. For information, see www.advisortoday.com.

Bloomberg Wealth Manager
This monthly magazine from Bloomberg L.P. focuses on the needs of financial advisers who work with the affluent. It is available for free to qualifying advisers. See wealth.bloomberg.com.

Financial Advisor
Written for independent broker-dealer representatives and registered investment advisers, this monthly publication should be on every adviser's reading list. Subscription details at www.financialadvisormagazine.com.

Financial Planning Magazine

An excellent all-around publication that covers the entire range of issues important to advisers. Subscription information and an extensive archive of past articles can be found at www.financial-planning.com.

Inside Information

We've found Bob Veres' newsletter, *Inside Information*, to be a great resource for keeping up with industry trends. Subscription information can be found at www.bobveres .com.

Investment Advisor

A monthly magazine serving advisers and planners, *Investment Advisor* pays particular attention to the needs of readers interested in the high-net-worth market. Subscribe at www.investmentadvisor.com.

Investment News

A weekly newspaper for advisers and brokers covering news from the entire financial services industry. Visit www .investmentnews.com for information.

National Underwriter

The only weekly magazine covering the life insurance, health insurance, and financial services industries, this publication focuses on identifying and analyzing the latest trends and developments for their significance to the market. For details, go to www.nationalunderwriter.com/ lifeandhealth.

On Wall Street

This monthly magazine focuses exclusively on stockbrokers and provides news, opinion, advice, and features, all aimed at helping readers attract and retain clients. For information, see www.onwallstreet.com.

Journal of Financial Planning

The official publication of the Financial Planning Association, this award-winning journal features prominent writers who cover all aspects of financial planning. To subscribe, visit www.fpanet.org/journal.

Registered Rep

A monthly publication covering practice management, investing, and wealth management. Find more details at www.rrmag.com.

Research

Published monthly, *Research* covers a broad range of issues for financial advisers, including financial planning, news, and trends in the industry and business development. For more information, see www.researchmag.com.

INDEX

ACAT (account transfer process), 189
account aggregation, 108
account viewing, by clients, 109
Acheson, Bill, 226
advanced consulting process. *See* consulting process, advanced
adviser(s)
    See also independent adviser
    client-centered, 82–86
    diagnostic meeting with, 71
    investment-centered, 82–84
    what affluent clients want in an, 47–52
affluent clients
    defined, 13, 45
    personal issues with, 48–49
    ratio of income and numbers of, 46
    reaching, 52–60
    what they want in an adviser, 47–52
affluent market
    growth of, 11–13
    levels of, 13–14
    needs of, 15–17
alliances
    See also referral partnerships
    building formal, 143–151
    commitment, 150–151
    compensation issues, 150
    components of, 136–138
    connections, establishing, 149
    documentation for, 149–150
    purpose of, 135
    success and, 135–136
    trust and respect in, 137

American Institute of Certified Public Accountants (AICPA), 223
Association for Investment Management and Research (AIMR), 223

Bachrach, Bill, 123, 225
banks, competition from, 24
bookkeeping, technology and, 109
Bowen, John, 123, 225–226
brand identity, 59
broker-dealer(s)
    alternative to, 166–167
    building a relationship with, 207–211
    deciding to change, 156–159, 171
    going independent and using, 206
    joining a large, 161–164
    joining a small, 164–166
    starting your own, 159–161
broker-dealers, changing
    client information, preparing, 187–188
    communicating about, 188–190
    depart from the old, 186–193
    gap when, 191–192
    lead time for, 186
    legal issues, 186–187
    relationship with the old, 192–193
    working with the new, 193–195
broker-dealers, evaluating
    backgrounds/culture, 172–174
    clearing firm, 180–181

compliance, 180
contacts, ongoing, 182–183
costs, 179–180
payout, 177
products, 174–175
Registered Investment Adviser,
181–182
services and support, 177–179
surprises, avoiding, 170–172
technology, 176–177

Cap Gemini Ernst & Young, 11
CEG Worldwide, research on, 4
alliances and success, 135–136
benefits of education, 118–119
client relationships, 49, 82–84
competition, 23–24
consultative approach, value of,
63
CPAs, 143–145
fee-based businesses, 64–65
growth of affluence, 12
income-client numbers ratio, 46
managing time, 95
planning and, 216, 217
prospecting strategies, 53–54
switching broker-dealers, 156
technology, 20
wealth management, 33–34
Central Registration Depository
(CRD), 195
clearing firm
conferences, 122
evaluating, 180–181, 208
switching broker-dealer and, 189
client-centered adviser, defined,
82–86
client communication
about broker-dealer switching,
188–190
consistent, 89
family meetings, 90–91
importance of, 86–87
language used, 92
methods of, 94, 110
methods preferred by client,
89

mistakes, handling, 93–94
personal, 88–90
responses from clients, providing methods for, 92–93
systematic, 87–88
technology and, 108, 110
client education
group seminars, 130–133
obtaining skills for conducting,
133
one-on-one methods, 129–130
purpose of, 127–128
client relationships, client-centered
versus investment-centered,
82–86
clients
See also affluent clients
for consultative process, 66–67
establish ongoing contact with,
73–75
prequalifying, 69
reminders, giving, 77
satisfaction and offering of
multiple services, 96–97
coaches/coaching programs, 107,
122–125, 225–226
commissions, 65, 166–167
commitments, obtaining
in alliances, 150–151
from clients, 76–77
communication
See also client communication
about broker-dealer changes,
188–190
with referral partners, 141–142
compensation, in alliances, 150
competition
changes in, 21–23
future for, 28–29
invisible, 24
media, impact of, 25–26
me e-generation, 26–27
types of, 23–24
compliance issues
broker-dealers and, 180
technology and, 110
confidentiality, 47–48

consolidation
    increase in, 38–39
    ups and downs of, 39
consultants, 226–228
consulting process, advanced
    commitments at every stage,
        getting, 76–77
    defined, 62–64
    diagnostic meeting with other
        advisers, 71
    discovery, 69–71
    fee-based, 64–65
    making the transition to, 78–80
    matching lifestyles and person-
        alities, 75–76
    ongoing contact, establishing,
        73–75
    presentation of capabilities,
        68–69
    presentation of recommenda-
        tions, 72
    presentation of staff, 77–78
    purpose of, 61
    reminders, giving clients, 77
    secure the agreement, 72–73
    selecting clients for, 66–67
    value of, 63
contacting clients, 73–75, 89
    See also client communication
contact management systems, 110
contacts, with broker-dealers,
    182–183
cost-benefit analysis of clients, 66
costs, broker-dealer, 159–160,
    170–171
CPAs, alliances with, 143–150
credibility, building, 58–59
customization, 50–51

Dent, Harry S., 130, 227
discovery step, 69–71
documentation
    in alliances, 149–150
    electronic storage and retrieval
        of, 109
    need for, 106

education, continuing, 110
    benefits of, 118–119
    business development track, 119
    coaches/coaching programs,
        107, 122–125
    from product wholesalers,
        126–127
    seminars and workshops,
        120–122
    study groups, 125–126
    technical issues track, 119
education for clients. See client
    education
employees
    feedback from, 106
    hiring, 105–106
    for managing the technology in
        your firm, 111–113
errors and omissions coverage, 179

family meetings, 90–91
fee-based consulting process
    defined, 64
    reasons for using, 64–65
fees
    commissions versus, 166–167
    initial, 76–77
Financial Planning Association
    (FPA), 121–122, 126,
    223–224

Gau, Tom, 226
Good, Bill, 87, 121, 227
Bill Good Marketing, 87, 227
Gregory, Kip, 227
group seminars, for clients, 130–133

hiring employees, 105–106

income-client numbers, ratio of,
    46
independent adviser
    broker-dealer relationship, 206
    deciding if you are ready to
        become, 198–201
    financial issues, 202–204
    legal issues, 202

preparation for becoming an,
201–206
institutional partners, outsourcing
and, 38
investment-centered adviser, 82–84
Investment Management
Consultants Association
(IMCA), 224

Junior Achievement, 133

Kolbe Corp., 105, 228

language used in communicating
with clients, 92
legal issues
when changing broker-dealers,
186–187
when going independent, 202
licenses, transferring, 195
listening, importance of, 59

magazines, 229–231
marketing
strategies, 55–57
technology and, 108, 110
mass affluent, 13
media, impact on competition,
25–26
me e-generation, 26–27
Merrill Lynch, 11
Million Dollar Round Table
(MDRT), 224
mistakes, handling, 93–94, 178, 179
Moeller, Steve, 123, 226
Monte Carlo simulation software, 115
Murray, Nick, 227–228
mutual funds, 99–101

NASD regulations, 110, 182, 189,
195
National Association of Insurance
and Financial Advisors
(NAIFA), 224–225
National Association of Personal
Financial Advisors (NAPFA),
224

National Association of Professional
Organizers (NAPO), 229
negative consent, 189
newsletters and newspapers, 58, 94,
229–231
niche opportunities
establishing your place within,
57–60
identifying, 56–57

order entry, 108
organizational chart, 105
outsourcing, 17
confidentiality and, 48
evolution of, 30–32
model, 34–36
need for, 33–34, 97–98
partners, 37–38
for single or multiple practitioner, 36–37

payout, broker-dealer, 177
performance statements, 106
Pershing, 122
planning software, 109
plans
importance of, 216–217
steps for implementing, 217–221
portfolio evaluation, 109
positive consent, 189
PowerPoint, 72, 131–132
Prince, Russ Alan, 4
presentation(s)
of capabilities, 68–69
PowerPoint, 72, 131–132
of recommendations, 72
of staff, 77–78
technology and, 108
products, broker-dealer, 174–175
product wholesalers, help from,
126–127
prospecting strategies, 53–54
Pusateri, Leo, 228

referral partnerships
See also alliances
building, 138–143

communicating with, 141–142
conduct between, 142–143
importance of knowing partners,
    139–140
matching clients with referrals,
    140–141
referrals, obtaining, 52, 53–54, 58,
    74
Registered Investment Adviser
    (RIA)
    broker-dealers and, 181–182
    pros and cons of becoming,
        166–167
reminders, giving clients, 77
research, technology and, 109
Roame, Chip, 228

sales, distinguishing between
    services and, 105
sales tactics, 59
Charles Schwab, 122
seminars
    for advisers, 120–122
    group, for clients, 130–133
services
    assessing potential, 101–102
    broker-dealer, 177–179
    client satisfaction and multiple,
        96–97
    distinguishing between sales
        and, 105
    offering the right, 96–102
    tips for providing, 102–197
    types of, wanted by clients, 98,
        99
significantly affluent, 13–14
Society of Financial Service
    Professionals, 225
Strategic Coach (Sullivan), 76, 105,
    123–124
strategic partners, outsourcing and,
    37
study groups, 125–126
Sullivan, Dan, 76, 77, 105, 123, 226
super affluent, 13
support, broker-dealer, 179

TD Waterhouse, 122
technology
    broker-dealer, 176–177
    employees to handle, 111–113
    future trends, 20–21
    how to get the most from, 108–
        115
    importance of, 18, 107
    problems with, 18–20
    selecting guidelines, 113–115
telephone systems, problem with
    computerized, 88–89
Tibergien, Mark, 228
tie-downs, 68
time log, use of, 107
time management, 106–107, 109
time re-engineering, 124
Toastmasters, 133, 229

ultra affluent, 13

value, 51

wealth management, 33–34
workshops, 120–122
World Wealth Report 2002, 11
Written Supervisory Procedures
    (WSP), 195

ABOUT BLOOMBERG

BLOOMBERG L.P., founded in 1981, is a global information services, news, and media company. Headquartered in New York, the company has nine sales offices, two data centers, and 94 news bureaus worldwide. Bloomberg, serving customers in 126 countries around the world, holds a unique position within the financial services industry by providing an unparalleled range of features in a single package known as the BLOOMBERG PROFESSIONAL® service. By addressing the demand for investment performance and efficiency through an exceptional combination of information, analytic, electronic trading, and Straight Through Processing tools, Bloomberg has built a worldwide customer base of corporations, issuers, financial intermediaries, and institutional investors.

BLOOMBERG NEWS®, founded in 1990, provides stories and columns on business, general news, politics, and sports to leading newspapers and magazines throughout the world. BLOOMBERG TELEVISION®, a 24-hour business and financial news network, is produced and distributed globally in seven different languages. BLOOMBERG RADIO℠ is an international radio network anchored by flagship station BLOOMBERG® 1130 (WBBR-AM) in New York.

In addition to the BLOOMBERG PRESS® line of books, Bloomberg publishes *BLOOMBERG® MARKETS* and *BLOOMBERG® WEALTH MANAGER*. To learn more about Bloomberg, call a sales representative at:

Frankfurt:	49-69-92041-0	São Paulo:	5511-3048-4500
Hong Kong:	852-2977-6000	Singapore:	65-6212-1000
London:	44-20-7330-7500	Sydney:	61-2-9777-8600
New York:	1-212-318-2000	Tokyo:	81-3-3201-8900
San Francisco:	1-415-912-2960		

FOR IN-DEPTH MARKET information and news, visit the Bloomberg website at **WWW.BLOOMBERG.COM**, which draws from the news and power of the BLOOMBERG PROFESSIONAL® service and Bloomberg's host of media products to provide high-quality news and information in multiple languages on stocks, bonds, currencies, and commodities.

ABOUT THE AUTHORS

CLIFF OBERLIN

The third generation of his family to manage a broker-dealer, Earl Clifford (Cliff) Oberlin III is CEO of Oberlin Financial Corp., a full-service financial advisory practice and broker-dealer.

Cliff served for many years as president and CEO of the family's first broker-dealer, MFI Investments, founded in 1959. MFI was named to the *Inc.* 500 fastest-growing privately held companies in the United States for three successive years beginning in 1993, before merging in 1995 with a multi-billion-dollar bank holding company, which today is known as Sky Financial, Inc. Together with Jill Powers and two other partners, he cofounded Oberlin Financial Corp. in 2000.

With more than twenty-five years experience as a licensed representative and general securities principal, Cliff has won numerous production awards, including life and qualifying member of the Million Dollar Round Table, Court of the Table, and Top of the Table honors. He has taken an active leadership role in industry organizations, having served as a member of the NASD District 8 (Chicago) Business Conduct Committee from 1994 to 1996, as chair of the NASD District 8 Business Conduct Nominating Committee, as chair of the International Association for Financial Planning's Broker-Dealer Division, and as a member of the Securities Industry Association's Independent Firms Committee.

He holds degrees in accounting and finance from Miami University (Oxford, Ohio) and holds a number of securities and insurance licenses. He is a Certified Public Accountant, Personal Financial Specialist, and Certified Financial Planner.

JILL POWERS

President of Oberlin Financial Corp., Jill Powers has a broad background in sales, financial planning, investment management, marketing, operations, and compliance. After working as an agency operations representative for Great American Insurance, Jill joined Cliff in 1993 to direct retail sales and service for MFI Investments (later known as Sky Investments). In 2000, Jill, Cliff Oberlin, and partners Tom Hofbauer and Steve Hess founded Oberlin Financial Corp. As president, Jill is responsible for directing the marketing, operations, and compliance divisions of the firm.

A Cum Laude and Phi Beta Kappa graduate of Miami University, Jill is also actively involved in the industry. She currently serves as chairperson of the NASD District 8 (Chicago) Business Conduct Committee and serves on the NASD Small Firms Advisory Board. She is also active in the Financial Planning Association in both the broker-dealer and the practitioner divisions. She holds several securities and insurance licenses and is a Certified Financial Planner.